WHY BOTHER?

The Riddle of the Good Samaritan

A traveling companion
for *Healing with Padre Pio*

Orest Stocco

WHY BOTHER?

Copyright © 2012 by Orest Stocco

All rights reserved. No part of this book may be reproduced or transmitted in any form or by any means without written permission of the author.

ISBN 978-0-9879357-3-1

Edited by Penny Lynn Cates
Cover Design by Penny Lynn Cates

*In loving memory of our mystical cat Hu-Lynn,
whose graceful transition taught me
how to let go with love.*

*"Fate is the death we owe to Nature.
Destiny is the life we owe to soul."*

BONE: Dying into Life

A Journal of Wisdom, Strength, and Healing

Marion Woodman

Table of Contents

Parable of the Good Samaritan 1
Prologue 3
1. The Riddle of the Good Samaritan 5
2. Inheriting Eternal Life 8
3. A Self-serving World 10
4. The Cost of a Smile 13
5. The Water of Everlasting Life 16
6. The Dawning of Self-consciousness 19
7. The Acorn Seed 22
8. The "I" of God 25
9. The Three Circles of Life 29
10. The Rich Young Man 31
11. The Mysteries of the Kingdom of Heaven 34
12. The Globe of Soul Fruit 37
13. What Goes Around Comes Around 39
14. Reincarnation Is Moot in Christ's Teaching 41
15. Sisyphus Is Not Happy 44
16. Heeding the Call 46
17. When the Student Is Ready 48
18. The Two Destinies of Man 52

19. There Are No Mistakes 56
20. The Three Stages of Evolution 59
21. The Way of All Ways..62
22. Why Do You Lie? 65
23. To Thine Own Self Be True 67
24. The Agnostic Christian..71
25. An Honest Persuasion..74
26. As Flies to Wanton Boys...76
27. Bought With a Price 78
28. On the Way to Jericho 81
29. The Selfsame Thing...85
30. The Soul's Real Code 89
31. A Jungian Slip 93
32. The Kingdom of Heaven 98
33. Keepers of the Flame...102
34. Letting Go and Letting God 105
35. Growth, Love, and Service..108
36. In Bad Faith 112
37. A Voyage of Discovery 114
38. The Great Slayer of the Real 116
39. The Selfish, Unselfish, and Selfless Self...................119
40. Why Bother?..121

Plus an Interview With the Author and More 124

Other Books by Orest Stocco

Coming Works

Parable

of the Good Samaritan

(Luke 10: 25-37)

"**And**, behold, a certain lawyer stood up, and tempted him, saying, Master, what shall I do to inherit eternal life?

And he said unto him, **What is written in the law? How readest thou?**

And he answering said, Thou shalt love the Lord thy God with all thy heart, and with all thy soul, and with all thy strength, and with all thy mind; and thy neighbor as thyself.

And he said unto him, **Thou hast answered right; this do, and thou shalt live.**

But he, willing to justify himself, said unto Jesus, And who is my neighbor?

And Jesus answering said, *A certain man went down from Jerusalem to Jericho, and fell among thieves, which stripped him of his raiment, and wounded him, and departed, leaving him half dead. And by chance there came down a certain priest that way; and when he saw him, he passed him by on the other side. And likewise a Levite, when he was at that place, came and looked on him, and passed by on the other side. But a certain Samaritan, as he journeyed, came where he was; and when he saw him, he had compassion on him. And he went to him, and bound up his wounds, pouring in oil and wine, and set him on his own beast, and brought him to an inn, and took care of him. And on the morrow when he departed, he took out two pence, and gave them to the host, and said unto him, Take care of him; and whatsoever thou spendest more, when I come again, I will repay thee. Which now of these three, thinkest thou, was neighbor unto him that fell among the thieves?*

And he said, He that showed mercy on him. Then said Jesus unto him, **Go, and do thou likewise.**"

Prologue

The Parable of the Good Samaritan is probably the best known of all of Christ's parables, and it does prick one's conscience; but why?

We would all like to live life on our own selfish terms, but somewhere along the way we realize that this is not always possible and we have to make concessions to our *higher nature*; this is what the Good Samaritan did when he stopped to help the injured man who was beaten by robbers and left for dead by the side of the road.

Jesus appealed to the cynical lawyer's *higher nature* when he answered his question, "Master, what shall I do to inherit eternal life?"

Jesus told him that if he wanted to inherit eternal life he would also have to make concessions to his *higher nature* and love his neighbor as he loved himself.

When I brought my novel *Healing with Padre Pio* to closure with the riddle of the Good Samaritan I was left in a quandary, because I honestly did not know what the riddle was. My Muse—the voice of my creative unconscious—offered the riddle to bring my novel to closure, but this riddle nagged at me for months until I could stand it no longer and decided to find out what my Muse was telling me.

I abandoned to the dialectical process of my creative unconscious and let my Muse work out the riddle of the Good Samaritan, but little did I expect that this would open the door to the mystery of Christ's secret teaching of eternal life, our *higher nature*.

When all is said and done, it's all about learning how to love; but what a journey it is to arrive at the simple truth that **God is love, and love is who we are!**

Orest Stocco,
Bluewater, Georgian Bay
June 1, 2012

1. The Riddle of the Good Samaritan

Although Padre Pio, the venerated Roman Catholic Saint and Ascended Spiritual Master who was channeled by a very gifted spiritual sensitive for my novel *Healing with Padre Pio*, told me that my novel was going to end with a question that would hold a mirror up to my reader, it still came as a surprise to me when I brought my novel to closure with the simple question, **Why bother?**

Oriano Felicci, who is my alter ego in my novel, told Lorie Anderson, a fledgling new member of the spiritual community that Oriano belonged to, that the path of love was the most difficult path in the world to live, and Lorie naively replied, "If it's so difficult, why would one bother?"

Smiling at her question, Oriano tells Lorie that she would have to earn the privilege for the answer to this question; but he gave her a clue. She could find the answer in the Parable of the Good Samaritan. And that's how my novel ended, with Oriano going his way and Lorie going off to solve the riddle of the Good Samaritan.

At the heart of the riddle of the Good Samaritan lies the central mystery of man's purpose in life, which Jesus reveals to the cynical lawyer in the parable; and man's purpose in life is what Jesus addressed and resolved with his teaching.

Jesus brought a teaching of salvation to the world, but salvation from what? The cynical lawyer asked Jesus what he had to do to *inherit eternal life,* and Jesus gave him the formula; but did he grasp the meaning of Christ's words?

The secret to *inheriting eternal life* lies in the riddle of the Good Samaritan, which the cynical lawyer may or may not have apprehended. This is why in the *Gospel of Thomas* Jesus said, **"Whoever finds the interpretation of these sayings will not taste death"**— meaning, one will *inherit eternal life* if he lived by Christ's teaching correctly.

Did the cynical lawyer realize that Jesus gave him the secret interpretation of his sayings with the parable? How many people know that what the Samaritan did for the injured man was the central message of Christ's teaching of *eternal life*?

When the priest saw the injured man on the side of the road he had two choices: (1), he could stop and help the man; and (2), he could walk on by. In effect, he asked himself, "Should I bother to help this man?" Or, as I phrased it in my novel to reflect the panoramic scope of the human experience—from bothering to scoop your dog poop to becoming a *sacred activist* and committing to an environmental cause to help save our planet: **why bother?** He chose not to bother.

Likewise, the Levite chose not to bother to help; but not the Samaritan. He stopped and helped the injured man, and he even walked the extra mile for him by paying the host at the inn to look after him until his return. The Samaritan chose to bother; but why?

Was the Samaritan simply a good person who saw a fellow human being in need of help and chose to help him? He could have walked away like the priest and Levite, but he did not. Why not? This is the riddle of the Good Samaritan.

"Many are called, but few are chosen," said Jesus; but what did Jesus mean by this cryptic comment? What does it mean to be called? And why are some people chosen and not others? And chosen for what?

Given the parable of the Good Samaritan, the answer is obvious: one is chosen for *eternal life*. What, then, made the Samaritan different from the priest and the Levite? What did the Samaritan have that would earn him *eternal life*, as the parable implies?

Again, Jesus reveals what he had: **compassion.**

The Samaritan showed mercy on the injured man, and he bothered to stop and nurse his wounds and transport him on his own animal to an inn and left instructions for the inn keeper to look after him, paying him for the service.

It follows that the Samaritan had what it takes to be chosen for *eternal life,* which was **love for his fellow man**; and when Jesus told the cynical lawyer to go and live his life as the Good Samaritan, he was telling him to grow in the consciousness of love and he would one day *inherit eternal life.*

But as obvious as the answer to the riddle of the Good Samaritan appears to be, the riddle is far from being resolved…

2. Inheriting Eternal Life

Jesus did not tell the cynical lawyer that he would be granted *eternal life* if he showed compassion for his neighbor; he told him that he would *inherit eternal life.*

This is the key to resolving the riddle of the Good Samaritan, because when we understand what Jesus meant by *inheriting eternal life* we will have the key to the right interpretation of his sayings.

One of the issues that I had to clear up with St. Padre Pio for my novel *Healing with Padre Pio* was the question of man's soul, because one of my teachers (Gurdjieff) did not believe that everyone is born with an eternal soul. St. Padre Pio replied that we are all sparks of Divine Consciousness, but some of us are not aware of it.

Indeed, he said, how can we not be eternal? We are all part of the Whole; hence we must all be a spark of Divine Consciousness. And our purpose in life is to grow in spiritual consciousness until we realize our divine nature.

By *inheriting eternal life* Jesus meant that we grow in spiritual consciousness by loving our fellow man like the Good Samaritan, but as Oriano told Lorie, "mastering the art of giving love is the most difficult thing in the world to do."

But why is it so difficult to give love? What compelled the priest and the Levite to walk away from the injured man? Obviously, they didn't want to bother; but why did they not want to bother?

Some inner force kept them from bothering, and they walked away leaving the injured man on the side of the road where he probably would have died had not the Samaritan

WHY BOTHER?

come by and showed him mercy. What, then, compelled the Samaritan to stop and help the injured man?

Jesus tells us that the Samaritan had compassion for the injured man. To have compassion is to have empathy, care, and consideration for others; so obviously the priest and the Levite did not have enough compassion to help the injured man.

It would have inconvenienced them to help. They were compelled by the force of their own character to walk away because empathy, care, and consideration for others were not an essential part of their character. They cared for themselves more.

This is the part of man's character that Jesus came into the world to save us from—our own selfish nature. Jesus knew that our selfish nature kept us from *inheriting eternal life*. This is why he said, **"He that loveth his life shall lose it; and he that hateth his life in this world shall keep it unto life eternal"** (John 12: 25).

This is the formula that unlocks the secret of Christ's sayings—*transforming the consciousness of our selfish nature*. This is how we solve the riddle of the Good Samaritan. This is why St. Padre Pio told me that the *selfless self* is what humanity strives for. This is how we *inherit eternal life*. But there's more to the riddle; much more…

3. A Self-serving World

Penny, my life companion of twenty-four years, flew out of Toronto to Thunder Bay last month to help her sisters tend to their father's precarious health. Penny's sister, who has been a registered nurse for years, was upset with the hospital for discharging their father, and she didn't think he had long to live; that's why Penny flew up to see her father. The call came at a bad time, but out of love for her father Penny, who is a Hallmark Rep, made arrangements with a co-worker to cover her stores while she was away.

She stayed a week with her father in his small apartment to tend to his failing health, which took some pressure off her sisters. She was not very hopeful that he was going to see his eighty-eighth birthday the following month, but a few days after she came home, sadly resigned to the fact that she had seen her father alive for the last time, her nurse sister finally managed to get their father admitted into a nursing home where he would have round the clock care; and by the grace of God his health began to improve. So much so, in fact, that he insisted the girls give him a party for his eighty-eighth birthday.

"I can't afford to make another trip up north so soon," Penny said one morning over coffee in my writing room. "He seems to be improving—"

"Sweetheart," I interrupted, "you'll regret it for the rest of your life if you don't go. Make the arrangements. We'll manage."

I had open-heart surgery three years ago and have been unable to work since, so our budget was very tight; but

WHY BOTHER?

filial love trumped budgetary concerns. Penny booked her flight, and I drove her to Barrie to catch the Go-Bus to Toronto very early in the morning three days before her father's birthday.

Her nurse sister picked her up at the airport and dropped her off at Lakehead Manor nursing home to be with her father, whose health was noticeably improving; and on Sunday they had their father's party at her other sister's larger home, with family and close friends attending, and Penny flew home much more resolved.

While waiting for her bus to pull into Barrie I sat in the depot and people watched, and I noticed an elderly woman preoccupied with her scratch-and-win cards when a man walked up to her and in a cheerful voice said, "Hi Lois. Are you waiting for someone?"

She looked up. "No, I'm catching the bus. You?"

"Yeah, me too," he replied, still cheerful.

"I sure hope I get a driver who smiles this time," she said.

"Oh," the man said, with some concern in his voice.

"They're so cranky these days," she amplified.

"I never really noticed," the man said.

"They could at least smile. It doesn't cost anything," she said, and went back to her scratch cards like she couldn't wait to see if she had won. The man stood for a moment or two longer but she never looked up again and he quietly walked away. Penny's bus pulled in and I walked out to wait for her to step off, smiling to myself at the woman's strange behavior. When Penny got off the driver stepped out to open the door to the luggage bin for her, but he made no effort to retrieve Penny's luggage. I reached in and pulled it out, and we went for lunch.

"I don't know what's with these bus drivers," Penny said, when I asked how her trip was. "A lady in Newmarket had to buy her ticket from the driver because she didn't have time to go into the depot, and he was very rude to her. And they don't help you with the luggage anymore. I don't know if it's a new policy, but they're not very accommodating."

"Why bother when they don't have to?" I said, with a snicker.

"They could at least smile. I watched some of the passengers get off the bus, and everyone thanked the driver on their way out; but he didn't say anything. He didn't even smile. They must be negotiating a new contract."

"Penny, it's a self-serving world out there, and people don't go out of their way for anyone if they don't have to. They don't even bother to smile if they don't have to."

"I know. Isn't that sad?"

4. The Cost of a Smile

Actually, Lois was wrong; it does cost to give someone a smile. And this speaks to the riddle of the Good Samaritan and mystery of Christ's teaching of *eternal life*, because giving a person a smile is also a gesture of love.

My teacher Gurdjieff taught me the "way of the sly man," which is the secret knowledge of how to catch the *life force*. People don't know it (not consciously, anyway), but they are forever giving and taking energy from each other; and, not only from each other, but from themselves as well.

Jesus taught this also. This is the secret knowledge of the Way. This is why Jesus told us to not let our left hand know what our right hand is doing when we give alms. This way we can store our "treasures in heaven." By "treasures" Jesus meant the precious *life force*. St. Padre Pio called Christ's "treasures in heaven" his "glory."

This is a very deep mystery that few people penetrate. Jesus called this mystery by many names. In the *Acts of John* in *The Apocryphal New Testament* he called it the word, the cross of light, the door, the way, the resurrection, the truth, seed, faith, Father, and kingdom of heaven, which he said was within; but what did he mean by this?

I knew what Jesus meant. That's why I said to St. Padre Pio when I went for my spiritual healing sessions with him for my novel *Healing with Padre Pio*, "Life is an individual journey"—because I had awakened to the Word within, which revealed its deepest secret to me that *life itself is the Way*.

St. Padre Pio, the humble Capuchin monk from Pietrelicina, Italy who embraced *la via di sofferenza* to *inherit eternal life,* understood me perfectly, and replied, **"Life is a journey of the self,"** because he knew that there is only self-initiation into the deep mysteries of the Way. But because the Way is the Way is the Way, we will all come to this realization eventually; as, for example, the seeker writer Hermann Hesse:

"It is a mysterious and yet simple secret known to the sages of all ages; the most minute act of selfless devotion, every act of compassion given in love makes us richer, whereas every effort towards possession and power weakens our strength and makes us poorer...Every time we act in the spirit of selflessness, out of loving sacrifice, our compassionate act of service, every renunciation of self-interest looks like a squandering, a self-deprivation and yet the truth is: such acts enrich us and make us grow. No other way leads forward and upward." (*Herman Hesse, The Seasons of the Soul.* translated by Ludwig Max Fischer, PhD)

But in today's hectic Facebook/Twitter world people are too preoccupied with the immediacy of their daily life to seek out the timeless secrets of the Way, despite pervading fears of an impending apocalyptic perfect storm, justifying their moral complacency that there is nothing they can do; but empty rationalizations cannot silence soul's divine imperative to realize its destiny of total self-realization consciousness, which Jesus referred to as *inheriting eternal life.* **"Seek ye first the kingdom of heaven, and all else will**

WHY BOTHER?

be given unto you," said Jesus, which he tells us how to do in the Parable of the Good Samaritan.

Reality is holographic, and any part of the Divine Matrix reflects the whole (Jesus said, **"I and my Father are one"**); that's why resolving the riddle of the Good Samaritan will gain one entry into the *kingdom of heaven*—meaning, the deep secrets of the Way.

But as Gurdjieff said to me when I began my quest for my true self, *"at first roses roses, then thorns thorns."* This is why living the path of love is the most difficult thing in the world to do.

5. The Water of Everlasting Life

I wrote a book called *What Would I Say Today If I Were To Die Tomorrow?* This autobiographical novel was inspired by a woman who was diagnosed with cancer and had only one year to live. She took advantage of her precious time and wrote a book for her children called *Before I Say Goodbye*. She wanted to tell her children everything that she had failed to tell them, for one reason or another; so her cancer gave her a golden opportunity to make peace with her family.

Her book struck a chord with me, and the idea possessed me to make my peace with the world; so I put myself under an imaginary sword of Damocles and wrote my own book in less than three months. And the first thing that I said I would say today if I were to die tomorrow was: **"We live more than one life, and it is foolish to deny this simply truth."** I said this because I believed in reincarnation.

I was born Roman Catholic, but my Christian faith could not contain me; so I became a spiritual seeker at a very early age. Like Hermann Hesse, who wrote the inspiring little allegory *Journey to the East,* I also travelled to the "East" to find my true self; but in my long and arduous journey I learned that one cannot find one's true self but has to instead *become* one's true self.

Gurdjieff taught me this truth with his remarkable teaching of "work on oneself," which opened the door to the transformative power of the enigmatic sayings of Jesus; and the more I *lived* the sayings of Jesus, the more I awakened to the Word within. The Word within is the *water of everlasting life:* **"But whosoever drinketh of the water that I shall give him shall never thirst; but the water that I shall give him shall be in him a well of water springing up into everlasting life"** (John 4: 14).

What is this miracle water? Because that's what one needs to *inherit eternal life*. Jesus tells us what it is in the Parable of the Good Samaritan. The injured man on the side of the road needed help, and the Samaritan showed compassion and nursed his wounds and saved his life. Obviously compassion is one of the ingredients of the miracle water of everlasting life. Still, that doesn't resolve the riddle of the Good Samaritan; but it lets us in.

Gurdjieff was a teacher of the Way. It was the Way according to Gurdjieff, though; and as much as his teaching did for me, I noticed that it lacked something. This something was **compassion**. So difficult was Gurdjieff's teaching to live by that it broke many students; but that's only because Gurdjieff had founded his teaching upon an incorrect perception of the human condition.

He believed that not everyone is born with an eternal soul, and with the help of his system of "work on oneself" one could create his own soul. This put a lot of pressure on his students. Most students eventually walked away; but I didn't.

I took Gurdjieff's teaching to the bittersweet end and gave birth to my eternal self in my mother's kitchen one summer day while she was kneading bread dough on the kitchen table. But I couldn't have done it without the sayings of Jesus.

So it was ironic that I had to leave my Roman Catholic faith to find the secret teaching of the Way in the

Word behind the words of Jesus. *"Verily, verily, I say unto you, If a man keep my saying he shall never see death,"* said Jesus (John 8: 51). And I thank Gurdjieff for waking me up to the Word behind the words of Jesus, because the more I "worked" on myself the more I *became* my true self; and the more I *became* my true self, the more I drank from the *well of everlasting life* and grew in spiritual consciousness until one fine day I shifted my center of gravity from my ephemeral outer self to my eternal inner self and gave birth to my spiritual self in my mother's kitchen!

I couldn't have done it without the *water of everlasting life*, though; which brings me back to the riddle of the Good Samaritan…

6. The Dawning of Self-consciousness

I discovered reincarnation in my teens, and in my twenties I read Jess Stearn's book *The Search for the Soul: Psychic Lives of Taylor Caldwell*, and I knew that one day I would write my own book on my past lives. That happened many years later when Penny and I moved to Georgian Bay, South Central Ontario. I had seven past-life regressions, and I called my book *Cathedral of My Past Lives*.

But even before I had my regressions I was convinced that I had lived before. I had three unforgettable past-life recollection dreams in my teens (one which was confirmed by one of my regressions, my lifetime in ancient Greece when I was a student of Pythagoras who taught the Way in secret), which is why I wrote in my novel memoir that the first thing I would say today if I were to die tomorrow is that we live more than one lifetime; but what does this have to do with resolving the riddle of the Good Samaritan?

Everything. But to make sense of this I have to reveal what happened to me during one of my past-life regressions. This regression was the key that opened the hidden door to the mystery of man's purpose in life.

It came as a shocking surprise to me. As I sank into the deep relaxation mode for my regression, I began to go back, and back, and back further, and further, and further until I went all the way back to where all souls come from—the Great Ocean of Love and Mercy, which is the Body of God!

I was an atom in the Body of God, but I did not have self-consciousness; I only had Soul consciousness. I knew that I did not have self-consciousness because I was observing and experiencing myself at the very ground of my eternal being in the Body of God; and after experiencing myself in the sweet bliss of God's Body, I felt myself being pulled down into the material body of my first primordial human life!

I was the alpha male of a group of ten or twelve higher primates, and I kept my clan in check with power grunts; that's why in my book *Cathedral of My Past Lives* I called myself "Grunt" in that lifetime. And then the most extraordinary thing happened in this regression that unlocked the mystery of life: *I experienced the actual dawning of my reflective self-consciousness!*

I did not have a reflective self until I gave birth to my reflective self. I had group consciousness but no self-consciousness, and after much deliberation and creative thought as I wrote the first draft of *Cathedral of My Past Lives* I finally worked out why I gave birth to my reflective self-consciousness—because of all the extra *life force* that I appropriated from my clan with my intimidating power grunts!

I had power over my clan members, and I exercised this power with brute force and power grunts. I always ate first and had sex whenever the urge possessed me; and every time I exercised my power they forfeited a little more of their *life force* to me. Their *life force* was their evolving individual will, and as I appropriated their will power I grew in my own individual will until I had individuated enough of their constellated will power to become aware of myself as a separate self!

That's how I gave birth to the reflective "I" of my consciousness. And this realization led me to see that the *life*

WHY BOTHER?

force is in essence the un-self-realized "I" of God, which led me to finally grasp what the Gnostics meant with their belief that we are all sparks of Divine Consciousness and that our purpose in life is to grow in spiritual consciousness until we become God-realized Souls—which the Gnostics taught with their secret teaching of the Way; and, to my great delight, which Jesus also taught with his teaching of the Way that he couched in his enigmatic sayings and parables!

"I am the way, the truth, and the life: no man cometh unto the Father but by me," said Jesus, who spoke for the Way (John 14: 6). Jesus lived the Way, which he had learned from the Essenes and his travels to the Far East, and he individuated the consciousness of the Way because life is an individual journey—just as Gurdjieff had individuated the Way, and my teacher Pythagoras had individuated the Way, and as anyone who lives the Way and grows in the consciousness of the Way individuates the Way because the Way is the *water of everlasting life* that flows through all life to nourish soul's *a priori* need for self-identity. But still, what does this have to do with the riddle of the Good Samaritan?

Again, everything…

7. The Acorn Seed

Gurdjieff said that Nature will only evolve man so far and then we have to take evolution into our own hands to realize our inherent potential; and Carl Jung, who came into my life by providential design when I hit another snag in my quest for my true self, said in an interview late in his life: *"As each plant grows from a seed and becomes in the end an oak tree, so man becomes what he is meant to be. He ought to get there but most get stuck."*

Jung spent his life helping people that were stuck on their journey through life, like the hopeless alcoholic Mr. Rowland H. who in turn inspired Bill Wilson to cofound the Society of Alcoholics Anonymous. His psychology of the self and brilliant grasp of the dreaming process freed people from their complexes and set them on their path to wholeness (Jung's analysis of Hermann Hesse helped the future Nobel Laureate through his state of depression, which he called "a mud hell"); but as luminous as Jung was in shining his light upon my path, his individuated consciousness of the Way fell short for me because he failed to take into account the karmic influence that our past lives have over us.

That's why I went to St. Padre Pio for a spiritual healing. I had one past lifetime that was so morally and sexually depraved (brought about by my vitriolic hatred for the Roman Catholic Church for what it had done to me) that I needed the sanctifying power of St. Padre Pio's healing grace to heal my wounded Christian soul and set me free.

WHY BOTHER?

Padre Pio suffered the holy wounds of Jesus for fifty years, and he grew in the consciousness of humility and compassion to such an astonishing degree that he openly declared, *"After death I will do more. My real mission will begin after my death,"* to which thousands of people throughout the world will attest, myself included.

Every year millions of people make a pilgrimage to his tomb in San Giovanni Rotondo, Italy because they seek his blessing; but I didn't have to go to Italy. I went to a spiritual healer forty kilometers from my home in Georgian Bay.

Once again, it was providentially designed to meet the woman who channeled St. Padre Pio for my novel *Healing with Padre Pio*; but however I came to meet her, I took advantage of the opportunity to clear up my issues with my old Roman Catholic faith whose dogmatic belief that we only live one life and that Jesus is the only true savior continued to fuel my past-life anger at Christianity.

Jung helped resolve my Roman Catholic *idée fixe* on evil with his breakthrough concepts of the shadow and Archetypal Shadow, but I still had to work through my deep-seated anger at the Holy Mother Church for condemning me to the rat-infested dungeon prison under the streets of Paris for "sowing the devil's seed" where I died a horrible death with a curse on my lips for God.

As Jung said, we are not born a *tabula rasa* because we're all genetically imprinted with our own distinct biology and patterns of behavior, but we also come into the world with our past-life histories. We all carry the memory of our former personalities in our personal unconscious, and they play an enormous role in determining our life's course—because the archetypal karmic patterns of our past lives affect the consciousness of our daily life. This is why the "Father of Holistic Medicine" Dr. Norman Shealy said in an interview: *"There is no other approach that I have experienced as effective as past-life therapy in getting people through lifelong and maybe multiple lives of problems."*

To which the man that Dr. Shealy was speaking with replied: *"It lets the human mind lift its boundaries and look wherever it needs to look for solutions for whatever bothers you; and, it doesn't come back. And that's the most valuable thing you can give anybody"*—just as the world's foremost clairvoyant Edgar Cayce did with the thousands of life readings that he gave for people around the world when he went into a deep trance and tapped into the Universal Mind for the answer to his client's life problems.

Taking evolution into our own hands means that we have to acknowledge the karmic reality of our past lives; otherwise we will continue to be plagued by the unconscious influence of the archetypal karmic patterns of our past life personalities that come into play in our daily life, as my past life personality as *"le salaud de Paris"* came into play in my current lifetime. I could never understand my lustful sexual urges until I had my past-life regression to my sexually depraved lifetime in Paris, and with St. Padre Pio's help I finally managed to resolve this life-long problem.

8. The "I" of God

My past-life regression to the Body of God and then to my first primordial human lifetime when I gave birth to my reflective self-consciousness gave me the missing pieces that I needed to solve the mystery of our purpose in life, and as I wrote *Cathedral of My Past Lives* I connected these missing pieces and worked out the Divine Plan of God.

No doubt there are many spectrums to the Divine Plan of God, but the one that I experienced awakened me to the evolutionary process of life. I came into the world as an un-self-realized atom of God (soul seed), and my purpose in life was to evolve in consciousness through the evolutionary cycles until I gave birth to a new "I" of God, or reflective self-consciousness. This was my human self, or ego consciousness.

In my first primordial human lifetime as "Grunt" I grew in ego consciousness by appropriating all the will power that I could get from my clan; and although it was a very dim self-awareness I knew that I was separate from my clan members, and I experienced loneliness for the first time in my existence.

From the moment I gave birth to my reflective self I began what Jung called the individuation of the constellated archetypal self. The *individuation process* is the growth and development of self-consciousness, and with each new incarnation I grew and evolved in personal self-consciousness.

I grew in self-consciousness through the natural process of karma and reincarnation; that is to say, now that I had given birth to a new "I" of God, as I lived my life I created personal karma, because you can only create personal karma when you have self-consciousness; and karma is soul's relationship with life.

This part of the puzzle took a long time to resolve, and I only resolved it when I connected the final missing piece—which, by luck (actually, it was also providentially designed) I just happened to have tucked away in the back of my mind. This was an experience that I had when I first began living Gurdjieff's teaching of "work on oneself" many years before I had my past-life regression back to the Body of God and my first human lifetime as "Grunt."

It was springtime, and I was sitting in the back yard of our family home, leaning back in my chair with my head touching the warm stucco of our house; and as I soaked in the soothing warm rays of the spring sun I closed my eyes and let my mind wander—and that's when it happened.

I felt myself drifting through time, back further, and further, and further; back through the ages, centuries, millennia, and eons—all the way back to when there was no life on Earth at all. I could see the planet Earth, and it was desolate and barren of all life; and I saw the gases of the Earth rise up into the sky, and as the gases blended with the gases from the sky they formed nuclei, which were amino acids, the first building blocks of life; and the moment the amino acids were created I felt myself "enter" into the emerging life process, and the moment I entered into the life process, LIFE WAS BORN!

I KNEW that by entering into the life process I experienced the very genesis of life on Earth, and it took a while to work out that what had entered into the life process of the forming amino acids was the un-self-realized "I" of God—meaning, the Soul consciousness of Divine Spirit.

Being an atom of God, I had Soul consciousness; and Soul consciousness is the un-self-realized "I" of God. When I "entered" into the life process as an atom of God, or soul seed, I imbued the emerging life process of amino acids with the I-consciousness of Soul—because, as I said, I just KNEW that the moment I became one with the life process I had initiated the very genesis of life on planet Earth; that is to say, the I- consciousness of Soul was responsible for the birth of life, *which led me to see that all of life is the un-self-realized "I" of God striving to give birth to God*—just as Meister Eckhart said: **"God is not blessed in his Godhead. He must be born in man forever!"**

Soul, which is made of Divine Spirit, is the consciousness of God, and Spirit is also the vital *life force* that creates and sustains life. This is how I reasoned out that the *life force* is the un-self-realized I-consciousness of God, because as an atom of God I did not have self-consciousness; I only had Soul consciousness. So by taking in the *life force* as I did in my primordial lifetime as "Grunt" by appropriating it from my clan members I took in the un-self-realized consciousness of God until I had taken in enough for it to become aware of itself—*and that's when I gave birth to a new "I" of God!*

With this final piece to the puzzle in place, I saw that the Divine Plan of God is all about God growing in the consciousness of God through the life process; which simply means that with every new "I" of God that life gives birth to, God grows in Divine Consciousness. This is how I came to the logical conclusion that the purpose of all life is to individuate the un-self-realized consciousness of God until

God gives birth to itself with each new "I" of God; but this is only the first stage of Soul's evolution through life. There are two more stages…

9. The Three Circles of Life

The three stages of soul's evolution through life are: the *exoteric*, or outer stage; the *mesoteric*, or middle stage; and the *esoteric*, or inner stage. In the first stage, soul evolves through life from the lowest life form up to the life form that will give birth to a reflective self-consciousness, as I did in my first human lifetime as "Grunt." Once soul has realized a matrix of reflective self-consciousness, it will grow in self-consciousness until it is ready for the second stage of evolution.

The first stage of evolution is governed by karma and reincarnation. Karma is the energy of life, and our karmic relationship with life is a relationship with the *life force*. The *life force* is the I-consciousness of Soul, and the more *life force* we take from life the more we grow in self-realization consciousness.

Although the *life force* is ours to have, it is not ours to keep; it belongs to life, which means that **the self that we create belongs to life.** This is why we all have a karmic relationship with life, and why Socrates said in Plato's *Phaedo*: "There is a doctrine uttered in secret that man is a prisoner who has no right to open the door of his prison and run away." *This prison is reincarnation.*

Once a soul enters into the life process it is trapped by life, and the only way out of the recurring cycle of life and death to get back home to God is *through* life—meaning, soul has to pay life back for the energy that it has taken from life to create a reflective self-consciousness; and learning how to pay life back for our reflective self-consciousness is what soul's journey through the *mesoteric* circle of life is all about.

Soul has no choice. It has to evolve through life until it learns the secret of how to break the endless cycle of karma and reincarnation. And learning this secret speaks to the riddle of the Good Samaritan, because by having compassion for the injured man on the side of the road the Good Samaritan stepped out of the *unconscious* first stage of evolution into the *conscious* second stage where he began to pay life back for all the *life force* that he had taken from life to create his own reflective self-consciousness.

This is the secret of *eternal life* that Jesus revealed to the world. Jesus told the cynical lawyer that he had to be like the Good Samaritan if he wanted to *inherit eternal life*; and by that he meant he had to pay life back for his own life, and the only way to pay life back was to sacrifice his life by giving his life back to life through love for his fellow man—which is why in my novel *Healing with Padre Pio* Oriano told Lorie that mastering the art of giving love was the most difficult thing in the world to do!

10. The Rich Young Man

In effect, in the first stage of evolution we take from life; and in the second stage of evolution we have to start giving back to life. Jesus revealed the secret of self-sacrifice to the rich young man in the *Gospel of Mark* (19: 16-24):

"And, behold, one came and said unto him, Good Master, what good thing shall I do that I may have eternal life?

And he said unto him, *Why callest thou me good? There is none good but one, that is, God; but if thou wilt enter into life, keep the commandments.*

But he said unto him, Which? Jesus said, *Thou shalt do no murder, Thou shalt not commit adultery, Thou shalt not steal, Thou shalt not bear false witness, Honor thy father and thy mother: and, thou shalt love thy neighbor as thyself.*

The rich young man said unto him, All these things have I kept from my youth up: what lack I yet?

Jesus said unto him, *If thou wilt be perfect, go and sell that thou hast, and give to the poor, and thou shalt have treasure in heaven: and come and follow me.*

But when the young man heard that saying, he went away sorrowful: for he had great possessions.

Then said Jesus unto his disciples, *Verily I say unto you, That a rich man shall hardly enter into the kingdom of heaven. And again I say unto you, It is easier for a camel to pass through the eye of a needle than it is for a rich man to enter into the kingdom of God.*"

Jesus was speaking metaphorically. By riches, he did not mean literal riches like gold and money and worldly possessions; he meant the riches of one's ego-consciousness. Ego is our reflective self, and our reflective self is made of the *life force* that life has given us to grow in self-consciousness—and the richer we are in ego consciousness, the harder it is to sacrifice our ego to gain *eternal life*.

"Whosoever shall seek to save his life shall lose it; and whosoever shall lose his life shall preserve it," said Jesus (Luke 17: 33). This is why Jesus said that many are called but few are chosen. The rich young man heard the call when he asked Jesus how he could gain eternal life, but he could not heed the call because he was too attached to his ego consciousness to sacrifice it for *eternal life*.

The rich young man still had to evolve through the *exoteric* first circle of life until life made him ready to heed the call to the *mesoteric* second circle of conscious evolution like the Good Samaritan, and life would make him ready through the unforgiving natural process of karmic reconciliation.

The *exoteric* first stage of evolution is all about creating and resolving karma. Karma is our relationship with life, which is positive and negative; meaning, we can *earn* the *life force* that we need to grow in self-realization consciousness, or we can *take* the *life force* from others through force, manipulation, guile, deceit, charm or whatever.

When we earn the *life force* that we get from life we are not obligated to pay it back to life. This is *positive karma*. And we earn *positive karma* through our own efforts and not by appropriating it from others. When we appropriate the *life force* from others we create *negative karma*, which must be paid back.

Jesus told the rich young man how he could create *positive karma* by keeping the commandments, but the rich young man said he had done this; and then Jesus told him that if he wanted to be perfect (meaning, if he wanted to *inherit eternal life*) he had to pay back the karmic debt that he owed life for all the *life force* that life had given him to create his rich and comfortable egocentric life.

The rich young man wasn't ready to sacrifice his life (ego) to save his life, and he walked away sorrowful because he didn't "hear" Christ's message. Which doesn't mean that he could not enter the *kingdom of heaven* (the *mesoteric* circle) simply because he was rich in material possessions; it means that he wasn't ready yet to sacrifice the rich consciousness of his ego self to realize the consciousness of his *eternal life*.

11. The Mysteries of the Kingdom of Heaven

Jesus gave his teaching to the public (the *exoteric* circle of life) in parables because the public wasn't ready yet for the secret teaching of the Way, but his disciples were; that's why they heard the call in Christ's teaching:

And the disciples came, and said unto him, Why speakest thou unto them in parables?
He answered and said unto them, **Because it is given unto you to know the mysteries of the kingdom of heaven, but to them it is not given.**
For whosoever hath, to him shall be given, and he shall have more abundance; but whosoever hath not, from him shall be taken away even that he hath.
Therefore speak I unto them in parables; because they seeing see not; and hearing they hear not, and neither do they understand. (Math. 13: 10-13)

What are these mysteries of the *kingdom of heaven* that the *exoterically minded* public could not hear? What was this secret knowledge that Jesus gave directly to his *mesoterically minded* disciples and to the public in parables?
Jesus called it being born again. This was the secret knowledge. **"Verily, verily, I say unto thee, Except a man be born again he cannot see the kingdom of God"** (John 3: 3). What, then, does it mean to be born again?
This is the core message of the secret teaching. Soul comes into the world an un-self-realized atom of God, and it evolves through life until it gives birth to a reflective self-

consciousness, as I did in my first human lifetime as "Grunt," and then soul continues to evolve through successive incarnations until life can evolve soul no further and we have to take evolution into our own hands.

This is the *exoteric* stage of evolution governed by the Spiritual Laws of Karma and Reincarnation. This is evolution through the consciousness of life and death, which is the consciousness of *being* and *becoming* that constitutes the focal point of our reflective self-consciousness, or ego self. Our inner self is our eternal self, but it is trapped in the consciousness of ego, and *"the only way out is through,"* as Robert Frost would say.

This is what Jesus meant by salvation. He taught the secret of how to free soul from the eternal cycle of life and death; and even though the public didn't understand the deeper meaning of Christ's teaching, it spoke to the *exoterically minded* soul on a level that it would understand—like the parable of the Good Samaritan. Everyone can grasp the moral of this parable, and it has been an inspiration from the day Jesus first told the cynical lawyer to go out and live his life like the Good Samaritan if he wanted to *inherit eternal life.*

Jesus taught the secret teaching of the Way, which is all about helping soul find its way out of the spiritual impasses of life that impede soul's journey back to God. When I was a student of Pythagoras in my past lifetime as Phaedrus, I was taught the secret teaching of how to free myself from myself by transforming the consciousness of my ego self by living a life of virtue. *"Be good, do good, and you will satisfy your longing for God,"* said Pythagoras.

The consciousness of ego is a consciousness of *being* and *becoming*, or as Sartre realized, *being* and *non-being*;

but ego consciousness is not pure enough for us to become aware of our eternal soul. This is why Sartre called man "a useless passion."

Sartre could not see the purpose of our existence, and he saw man trapped in the life process of *being* and *non-being*, hence his famous play *No Exit*. *"I am what I am not, and I am not what I am,"* he declared, summing up his philosophy; but that's only because he didn't know how to free himself from himself.

"For whosoever will save his life shall lose it," said Jesus, which Socrates echoed in the *Phaedo*: *"For I deem that the true disciple of philosophy is likely to be misunderstood by other men; they do not perceive that he is ever pursuing death and dying..."*

By "true disciple of philosophy" Socrates meant the soul that has been called to the Way, as Christ's disciples were called because they were ready to enter into the *mesoteric* second stage of evolution, which Jesus called *kingdom of heaven* where they learned how to take evolution into their own hands and free themselves from themselves.

This is the secret of *eternal life* that Jesus revealed in the Parable of the Good Samaritan, and which by the grace of God I realized in my mother's kitchen; and having "died" to my life to "find" my life I was able to complete the *individuation process* that Jean Paul Sartre left incomplete: *"I am what I am not, and I am not what I am; I am both, but neither: I am Soul!"*

12. The Globe of Soul Fruit

As the acorn seed *has to become* an oak tree, so every soul seed *has to become* what it is meant to be—a God-realized Soul Self; but because every soul creates its own personal karma, no two souls will create the same Soul Self.

Personal karma determines our spiritual path in life. This is why St. Padre Pio told me that life is a journey of the self. No two selves walk the same path. We may walk the same outer path (like Christianity, Buddhism, or Sufism), but no two souls walk the same karmic path—because soul's karmic relationship with life is unique to each and every soul.

In the Sufi Allegory *The Conference of the Birds,* thousands of birds (souls) went on a quest for God. The Hoopoe Bird was their guide. The quest for God was long and arduous, and only thirty birds succeeded. And when these thirty remarkably courageous birds looked into the Face of God they saw their own image!

Although every bird was different from one another but still a bird, when they looked into the Face of God they saw their own individuated Soul Self, which was God-realized. *"These leaves, our bodily personalities, seem identical, /but the globe of soul fruit we make, /each is elaborately unique,"* said the mystic Sufi poet Rumi.

This is the mystery of spiritual self-realization consciousness that Jesus addressed when he said, **"I and my Father are one."** Jesus was one of the blessed birds that looked into the Face of God and saw his own Soul Self, and like the Hoopoe Bird that guided the birds back home to God so too does Jesus guide souls to the *kingdom of God* with his teaching of spiritual rebirth.

"I, you, he, she, we, /In the garden of mystic lovers, /These are not true distinctions," said Rumi, drawing the distinction between our karmic self (ego), and our spiritual self (Soul), telling us that although our "bodily personalities" may be different, the "globe of soul fruit" we make is unique; and making this "globe of soul fruit" is what the Parable of the Good Samaritan speaks to.

13. What Goes Around Comes Around

The *exoteric* circle of evolution is all about acquiring enough *life force* to create a reflective self-consciousness; consequently, it is a very primal, aggressive stage of evolution. The primary purpose of this first stage of evolution is survival, and mastering survival defines the nature of the reflective self.

"It's a dog-eat-dog world out there," says the man in the marketplace, reflecting the general ethic of the *exoterically minded* survivor. He is not aware yet of the Spiritual Laws of life that govern his outer spiritual path; but aware or not, his spiritual destiny is governed by his personal karma.

How one acquires his *life force* determines the course of his spiritual path, because the more one appropriates the *life force* from the world the more karma he will have to pay back to life; consequently, he perpetuates the archetypal patterns of his karmic destiny—until one day it dawns upon him that *what goes around comes around,* and he will see that he is the author of his own misery.

"It's a jungle out there," says the *exoterically minded* man; and he has to be strong willed to survive in the world. Effectively then, the self that one acquires in the outer circle of life is a very primal and selfish self driven by power, because power facilitates survival; and it's very hard to go against one's primal nature and go out of one's way to help an injured man on the side of the road, like the Good Samaritan did.

As the saying goes, *"a zebra cannot change its stripes."* If one is selfish by nature, it is very hard for him to go against his nature; which is why people can be so predictable. But we are free to change our nature by changing our consciousness; and as we change our consciousness, we change our spiritual destiny. Andrew Harvey calls this *sacred activism.*

Jesus brought a radical teaching of *sacred activism* into the world to help man change his selfish nature so he can change his *karmic destiny*. When Jesus told the cynical lawyer to go and have compassion for his fellow man like the Good Samaritan, he was telling him that he had to change his nature to *inherit eternal life*. It was his choice; he could be like the priest and Levite, or he could be a *sacred activist* like the Good Samaritan and change the course of his *karmic destiny* by having compassion for his fellow man.

But as Jesus tells us with the parable of the rich young man, it's hard to become a *sacred activist*. The *exoterically minded* rich young man did not want to give up his earthly possessions—which isn't what Jesus was talking about at all. Jesus wanted the rich young man to give up the habits of his selfish nature and follow him. And by following him, Jesus meant that he had to live the *way of self-sacrifice* that he had introduced into the world to free man from the karmic patterns of selfishness that perpetuate the cycle of life and death; that's what Jesus, the world's most famous *sacred activist*, meant by salvation!

14. Reincarnation Is Moot in Christ's Teaching

It always puzzled me why Jesus made little reference to reincarnation in his teaching, but as I was working on *Healing with Padre Pio* I came to understand why. But first I had to establish with St. Padre Pio that we live more than one life, to which he readily assented. I knew that this would be another point of contention with the Roman Catholic Church that had canonized him, but he didn't mind. *"This is what the world needs at this time,"* he said, no longer constrained by Catholic dogma, *"a new way of thinking."*

The truths we live by determine our life, but what if the truths we live by are founded upon false premises? Gregg Braden addresses this disturbing question in his book *Deep Truth*, stating that modern man is living according to scientific truths that are fundamentally flawed and that these truths have brought the world to the brink of apocalyptic disaster; but flawed or not, whatever truths we live by life still comes down to a journey of the self, and it is man's responsibility to realize his *spiritual destiny*. As Padre Pio told me in one of my spiritual healing sessions, "Life is about GROWTH and UNDERSTANDING."

Once I realized that Christ's teaching was all about liberating soul from the illusion of time and space (the recurring cycle of life and death), I UNDERSTOOD that reincarnation was moot in Christ's teaching—because it didn't' matter if one lived in the year 100, 1245, or the year

2012 Christ's teaching addressed the liberation of soul from one's karma—*regardless which lifetime one lived!*

To make the point, St. Padre Pio revealed something about my life that shocked me out of my old way of thinking about reincarnation. (Gregg Braden quotes Albert Einstein saying that *"a new way of thinking is essential if mankind is to survive and move toward higher levels."*) Speaking from "a place of all knowing and all seeing," the Ascended Spiritual Master St. Padre Pio told me that I have relived my same life over again three separate times, and this was one of those lives.

Apparently I wasn't satisfied with the outcome of my first lifetime as Orest Stocco, and I returned to relive my same life over again to obtain a different outcome. I was closed-minded about "that other religion" the first time I lived my same life, but this time I am open-minded about it; enough so, in fact, that I have been living "that other religion" for the past thirty-five years now!

So there is much more to reincarnation than meets the eye, as there is with karma as well because the Good Saint told me also that karma is soul's choice and that a soul could live life without karma. I didn't understand what he meant by this, but I'm working on a new book that is opening the door to this mystery—which seems to be the "acorn seed" of my life, to borrow a phrase for my *karmic destiny* from James Hillman.

The point being that it doesn't matter what truths we live by, if they are false they will lead us to a dead end, and it's up to us to find our way out; and if we can't find our way out Divine Spirit, the omniscient guiding force of life, will always step in and point the way for us; but it's up to us to take the new direction. And this is what the parable of the

WHY BOTHER?

Good Samaritan speaks to: **why bother?** We can be a *sacred activist* and have compassion for our fellow neighbor, or we can choose not to bother; it's entirely up to us.

So it doesn't matter which life we live. It could be my respected life as a politician in Athens in ancient Greece, my imbalanced life as a Sufi in medieval Persia, my debauched life in Paris, France, my insufferable life as a black slave in southern Georgia, or my life in Genoa, Italy as a "man of the world" —whatever life we live there will always be an injured man by the side of the road, and it will always be our choice to help him or not. That's why reincarnation is moot in Christ's teaching, because his call to spiritual liberation is the same for all time. But do we have "ears" to hear Christ's call to *sacred activism*?

15. Sisyphus Is Not Happy

The reason we have such a confused understanding of our purpose in life is because we have two destinies: one karmic and one spiritual; and until we align our two destinies we will always remain confused.

"The struggle itself is enough to fill a man's heart. One must imagine Sisyphus happy," said the atheist philosopher Albert Camus in his book of essays *The Myth of Sisyphus*, but I could not comply. Camus' philosophy of the absurd was a dead end, and I had to find my way out of this despairing philosophical impasse.

Sisyphus offended the gods and was condemned to Hades to rolling a huge rock up a hill whence it would roll back down of its own accord. He had to roll it back up again, and again, and again. He had to do this for eternity. Camus used this ancient myth as a metaphor for the soul-destroying grind of man's daily life. As a friend of mine once said, *"we work and then we die."* And what's the point of it all?

Once again, the truths that we live by determine the course of our life; and if we live by a truth that denies we have an immortal soul that lives more than one life and that we are here to grow into who we are meant to be and then die and cease to be, then life can become "a tale told by an idiot full of sound and fury signifying nothing."

And if we live by a truth that tells us that if we die in a state of mortal sin we will be condemned to hellfire for eternity, we live in a state of fear and dread. *"Thou shalt not commit adultery,"* the Seventh Commandment tells us; but

WHY BOTHER?

what if I fall in love with a married woman and commit adultery; what then?

I go to confession and my parish priest absolves me of my sin, but I'm still in love with the married woman and I commit adultery again and I go to confession again and my parish priest absolves me again; but I'm not free. I'm trapped between my love for a married woman and my Roman Catholic faith, and I am torn by love and dread.

"How can a love that makes me feel so good be a sin?" The whole concept of sin bothered me, and I had to find a way out of my dilemma. I felt like a gerbil on a treadmill—sin and confession, sin and confession, sin and confession, a never-ending Sisyphean struggle that so tried my soul I had to find a solution. I could not imagine Sisyphus happy, and I dropped my faith to look for a way out of my dilemma!

16. Heeding the Call

It takes courage to let go of one's truth. But life is inherently self-correcting. This is the nature of karma. Life gives us the experiences we need to test our truth, and if we pass the test a new truth opens up to us.

My new truth was the ancient teaching of karma and reincarnation, and my test was letting go of my old Roman Catholic truth that we only live one life that Jesus died on the cross to save for us.

I passed the test and embraced my new truth, but my new truth cost me dearly because I left my Roman Catholic faith with tons of repressed guilt and anger; that's why I went for a spiritual healing with St. Padre Pio.

When Padre Pio was alive he accepted his Roman Catholic faith with his whole heart and soul. He believed in sin and forgiveness of sin. But he sees things differently from the Other Side now. He knows that soul lives more than one life (in fact, he told me that he is living in another body today as a Catholic priest in El Salvador, which should make the Roman Catholic Church stand up and take notice), and that from his place of all knowing and all seeing sin does not exist, as such.

Life is all about experience, and there is no right or wrong way to live life because essentially life is all about GROWTH and UNDERSTANDING. But what is this precious UNDERSTANDING that we are here to learn? This was my "acorn."

I had to find my path in life. I was born *mesoterically minded*, but I grew up in a family that was *exoterically centered*; and my life was very confusing. I did not fit in with my family, friends, or society at large; and I became a seeker at an early age.

I found the Way, and I began to understand my purpose in life; but to arrive at this precious UNDERSTANDING I had to bring my outer *karmic destiny* into alignment with my inner *spiritual destiny*, and this was very hard.

I read a poem in my youth that speaks my struggle aligning my *karmic destiny* with my *spiritual destiny*. Cleanthes, the ancient Greek Stoic philosopher/poet, wrote:

> Lead me, o Zeus
> And thou o destiny
> The way I am bid by thee to go;
> To follow I am willing,
> For were I recusant
> I do but make myself a slave
> And still must follow.

My problem was that I wasn't willing to follow, and I made myself a slave to my soul's destiny; hence, I was dragged by my *spiritual destiny* and suffered so much that I cursed my gods of fate more times than I care to remember. But life wore me down, and I finally gave up and heeded the Call of my *karmic destiny*.

17. When the Student Is Ready

There's an old saying, *when the student is ready the teacher appears*; but the teacher can take many forms. The teacher can come by way of an experience, a meaningful coincidence, a book, or an actual person; and the teacher always addresses one's state of consciousness accordingly.

My first teacher came to me by way of an explosive daemonic poem that I wrote in high school called "Noman." (I'm exploring my parallel life in the new book that I am writing called *The Summoning of Noman,* because I believe this poem was my point of entry into my parallel life.) And my teacher appeared again shortly thereafter by way of literature. I was so moved by Somerset Maugham's novel *The Razor's Edge* that I wanted to be like Maugham's hero Larry Darrel.

Larry Darrel had a deep longing to understand the meaning and purpose of life, and he walked away from his fiancé and friends and society to become a truth seeker. His commitment gave me the courage to become a seeker also, and I expanded my reading to include the spiritual literature of all cultures, and I became a voracious reader. And by the time I went to university to study philosophy I was ready to meet my teacher in person, in a matter of speaking that is, because I met G. I. Gurdjieff through P. D. Ouspensky's book *In Search of the Miraculous: Fragments of an Unknown Teaching.*

Shortly after I devoured this book I met Gurdjieff in person in a dream and I boldly asked him to accept me into his inner circle of students, but he said I wasn't ready yet.

WHY BOTHER?

After two years of "working" on myself I met him in a dream again, and this time he accepted me into his inner circle. Outwardly I read all the books on his teaching that I could lay my hands on (I had to order them from *Samuel Weiser Inc.* in New York), and inwardly he came to me at critical periods in my dreams to teach me "the way of the sly man."

As I "worked" on myself I brought my *karmic destiny* into alignment with my *spiritual destiny*; so much so, in fact, that I outgrew Gurdjieff's teaching and had to move on to another path more suited to my new state of consciousness, and I found what St. Padre Pio delicately referred to as "that other religion" that I was closed-minded about the first time I lived my life as Orest Stocco. But when I met the spiritual leader of "that other religion" in a dream one night, I said to him, "What do I call you?"

I did not want to call him my Spiritual Master because I had a bad taste in my mouth for Spiritual Masters after my traumatizing experience with an offshoot Christian solar cult teaching that did irreparable physical damage to my eyesight (although I was living Gurdjieff's teaching, I was forever exploring new paths); but he did not answer me. He just smiled and put his arm around my shoulder and turned me around, and as I turned I found myself staring into the Face of God!

It took two years before it dawned on me that the spiritual leader of "that other religion" was a God-realized Soul, and thirty-five years later I'm still living "that other religion" because it satisfies my need to UNDERSTAND.

"That other religion" is an ancient spiritual teaching brought out into the modern world in 1965 (essential principles of this spiritual path can be found in the Essene teachings, Gnosticism, Alchemy, Sufism, Taoism, and Jung's *process of individuation* to name the most obvious paths). It is said to be "the most direct path to God," and if one has a spiritual need for this path he will find it because this is how life works.

"There is more than one way," said St. Padre Pio, because the Way is holographic and all ways reflect the Way, and we will always find the path best suited to our individual state of consciousness. My consciousness brought me to "the most direct path to God," and I was privileged to look into the Face of God.

This did not grant me instant enlightenment, though; far from it. All it did was fill me with so much spiritual conceit that it took the devastating power of St. Padre Pio's humility to slay the beast of my unconscious vanity; which led me to the sobering realization that **ultimately our life is a journey through vanity to humility**, and not until we resolve the riddle of the Good Samaritan will we be free of our own ego.

The romantic poet Shelly saw man's journey through vanity to humility, and he captured it in his ironic poem *Ozymandias*:

> I met a traveler from an antique land
> Who said: Two vast and trunkless legs of stone
> Stand in the desert. Near them, on the sand,
> Half sunk a shattered visage lies, whose frown,
> And wrinkled lips, and sneer of cold command,
> Tell that its sculptor well those passions read
> Which yet survive, stamped on these lifeless things,
> The hand that mocked them and the heart that fed;
> And on the pedestal these words appear:

WHY BOTHER?

"My name is Ozymandias, king of kings:
Look on my works, ye Mighty, and despair!"
Nothing round remains, boundless and bare
The lone and level sands stretch far away.

18. The Two Destinies of Man

What does it mean to have two destinies? *"Vanity of vanities, sayeth the Preacher, vanity of vanities; all is vanity. What profit hath a man of all his labor which he taketh under the sun?"* (Eccl. 1: 2-3)

The Preacher references our karmic purpose in life, which makes no sense at all if one does not accept reincarnation as a fact of life. The Preacher alludes to reincarnation—*"One generation passeth away, and another generation cometh; but the earth abideth for ever...All the rivers run into the sea; yet the sea is not full; unto the place from whence they come, thither they return again...There is no remembrance of former things"* (Eccl. 4,7,11)—and he concludes his inquiry on man's purpose in life with basically the same advice Jesus gave to the rich young man who wanted to know the secret of *eternal life*:

"And further, by these be admonished: of making many books there is no end; and much study is a weariness of the flesh. Let us hear the conclusion of the whole matter: Fear God and keep his commandments: for this is the whole duty of man. For God shall bring every work into judgment, with every secret thing, whether it be good, or whether it be evil" (Eccl. 12: 12-14).

Meaning: we cannot run away from our own karma and will one day have to align our *karmic destiny* with our *spiritual destiny*. St. Paul said, *"Be not deceived; God is not mocked: for whatsoever a man soweth, that shall he also*

WHY BOTHER?

reap" (Gal. 6: 7). And after many years of looking for my true self, I came to the same conclusion; but I expressed it according to the dynamic of my own spiritual quest: **the purpose of life is to simply be a good person.**

In effect, I had solved the riddle of the Good Samaritan in my realization that to align my *karmic destiny* with my *spiritual destiny* I had to transform the consciousness of my selfish ego, and the most effective way to do that was to do good, and be good—*which was the most demanding discipline of my entire life!*

Gurdjieff's teaching of "work on oneself" had awakened the Word in me, which opened up the enigmatic sayings of Jesus like the petals of a rose, and the more I *lived* the sayings of Jesus the more I grew in the realization that Gurdjieff's teaching lacked the most essential ingredient for "creating" one's own soul—*love*. And the best and most efficient way to get the energy of love was to be a good person; so I made the virtue of goodness central to my personal ethic.

That's how I solved the riddle of the Good Samaritan; and getting to this point is what my journey through the *mesoteric* circle of life was all about. I had to transform the consciousness of my lower self by mastering the art of giving love—meaning, I had to discipline myself to stop and help the injured man by the side of the road.

This is why I always picked up hitchhikers whenever I travelled to the north shore communities of North Western Ontario for my work as a drywall taper and painting contractor—from my hometown of Nipigon north to Thunder Bay, east to Long Lac, and south to Terrace Bay and as far as Manitouwadge—and more often than not assisting them with some money for a meal, or a bus ticket to their next destination.

I picked up a woman one summer day on my way back to Nipigon from Thunder Bay where I had gone to pick up painting supplies who made such a powerful impression upon me that to this day I am still moved to tears of compassion—*because her whole life spoke soul's inherent longing for God!*

She was in her middle to late thirties, neatly dressed in a pair of blue jean coveralls over a clean patterned shirt, carrying a knapsack on her back. She was a graduate nurse who for one reason or another left her work and decided to see the country, Jack Kerouac-like, with no destination in mind.

Leery at first, as well she should be because who knows what kind of people are going to pick up a hitchhiker, especially a good-looking woman, she finally warmed up to me and told me a little about herself; but as we talked I couldn't help but get the strongest feeling that she was a lost soul, and my heart automatically went out to her.

She had no home of her own, nor a home to go to, and I couldn't help but feel that she was travelling across the country in search of a place to be; that's when I shared my spiritual path with her in the hope that it would help her find her way back home to God where I felt she longed to be.

I dropped her off at the Husky Restaurant in Nipigon, giving her twenty dollars for a meal and a card with the name of my spiritual path and prayer that would help her find her way, and I wished her the best of luck; and as I drove away I waved goodbye and she had such a look of gratitude in her bewildered eyes that a flood of goodness

WHY BOTHER?

washed over me, and I thanked my lucky stars for the precious gift of love she had given me.

19. There Are No Mistakes

"All life is reduced to one task: surrender of ego," said Marion Woodman, a Jungian analyst, in her book *Bone: A Journal of Wisdom, Strength, and Healing*; but it often takes a harrowing life experience to bring us to this realization. And this is always brought about naturally by the inherently corrective nature of karma, as Marion Woodman's journey through her uterine cancer experience illustrates.

This is the mystery of our two destinies. We come into the world as a soul seed, an atom of God that is pre-scripted to become God-realized; but **we can only realize our spiritual destiny through our karmic destiny**, which is why we will keep coming back again and again until we get life right.

Soul does not have self-identity. Soul is the un-self-realized consciousness of God, and to acquire self-identity we have to go through the natural process of evolution to individuate the consciousness of God.

Evolution—the natural process of life and death—is governed by the Spiritual Laws of Karma and Reincarnation; hence, soul creates its own *karmic destiny* by the choices it makes. This is why St. Padre Pio told me that **there are no mistakes, only bad choices**; and a bad choice is one that creates karma that takes soul away from its pre-scripted *spiritual destiny*. This is why Marion Woodman said in her book *Bone*: *"Fate is the death we owe to Nature. Destiny is the life we owe to soul."* This is the paradoxical nature of our *karmic destiny* that leads to death and our *spiritual destiny* that leads to *eternal life.*

In a moment of acute poetic insight, the Romantic poet John Keats caught a rare glimpse of the Divine Plan of God in a letter that he wrote to his brother, titled "The Vale of Soul-making." Nowhere does his genius shine more brightly:

"There may be intelligences or sparks of divinity in millions, but they are not Souls till they acquire identities, till each one is personally itself. Intelligences are atoms of perception—they know and they see and they are pure; in short, they are God. How then are Souls to be made? How then are these sparks which are God to have identity given them—so as even to possess a bliss peculiar to each one by individual existence? How but by a medium of a world like this?" (*Values*, edited by J. G. Bennett)

This defines man's most fundamental need—*self-identity.* It is not air, water, food, sex, power, or love even—it is self-identity. Man is born with an *a priori* need for self-identity, because every soul is pre-scripted to become God-realized, and it can only become God-realized through the *individuation process* of life and death—*hence, man's irrevocable a priori need for self-identity.*

My greatest need was to be myself, as is every person's greatest need to be himself or herself; but herein lies the mystery of the *individuation process*, because to be who we are meant to be—one whole, integrated self—we have to transform the consciousness of our ego self; and this no one wants to do willingly.

But we have no choice, because soul is teleologically driven to realize its divine nature; which means that we will always be dragged by our *spiritual destiny* if we make choices that are not in agreement with our spiritual purpose. This is why the Sufis say that there are as many paths to God as there are souls of man, because each soul has to realize its destiny through its own *individuation process*, which is why St. Padre Pio said in one of my spiritual healing sessions: "Life is a journey of the self."

20. The Three Stages of Evolution

"My life is a story of the self-realization of the unconscious," said Carl Jung, the Swiss psychoanalyst who courageously parted the veil of life and gave us a glaring look at the mystifying process of self-individuation, and the study of dreams was the path that he chose to satisfy his greatest need:

"By following the messages appearing in dreams, Jung believed that the path leading to self-realization and personal wholeness could be discovered. His belief was affirmed in a dream he experienced just before his death. In it he saw, 'high up in a high place,' a boulder lit by the full sun. Carved into the illuminated boulder were the words" *'Take this as a sign of the wholeness you have achieved and the singleness you have become.'"* (*Our Dreaming Mind*, by Robert L. Van de Castel)

So acutely conscious did Jung become of the *individuation process* by "confronting the unconscious" and studying *the way of the dream* that he came to the realization that dreams could be considered to be a meeting place between all that an individual had been in the past (including past lives) and all that he might be in the future (written in his soul's code), and he took dream messages very seriously, especially his own, because dreams are soul's message to the conscious mind on how to realize our *spiritual destiny*.

The way of the dream was Jung's path to wholeness and singleness of self, which he realized near the end of his life; but just because Jung had brought his outer self into agreement with his inner self didn't mean that he had realized his *spiritual destiny* yet; that's why he came to me in a dream to talk about my book *The Way of Soul*.

Jung was still puzzled by the *individuation process*. He wanted to know all he could about what he called "the alpha and omega of the self," and we talked for hours in my dream about *The Way of Soul,* which was not even transcribed yet on this side of the veil. All the tapes of my "Soul talk" book were still neatly stored in a cookie tin on the bottom shelf of one of my bookcases; but time is different on the Other Side.

The point being: Jung took *the way of the dream* to integrate his outer and inner self, and I took *the way of Soul* to integrate my two selves. Jung did not consciously pursue "death and dying" ("die before dying," as the Sufis define *the way of the Sufi*), to bring his two selves into agreement, but I did; that's why I suffered so much—because it is very, very painful to consciously transform the selfish consciousness of one's ego. This is why I told St. Padre Pio that I wouldn't wish Christ's teaching upon anybody, because *the way of Christ* is all about "losing one's life to find one's life."

Self-sacrifice is the central message of Christ's teaching, which Padre Pio embraced by taking *la via di sofferenza* when he took the vows of his Capuchin Order; and so passionately did he embrace *the way of suffering* that he could not suffer enough. *"I want to inebriate myself with pain,"* he said; and, God bless him, he did manage to realize his divine nature and now helps souls find their way from the Other Side.

WHY BOTHER?

He was too humble to tell me that he had attained spiritual ascendancy, but he revealed himself when he told me that he now spoke from a place of "all knowing and all seeing"—which meant that he was one with Divine Spirit now.

So just because one manages to bring his outer self into agreement with his inner self does not mean that the journey of the self is over; far from it, because there is no end to spiritual self-realization and God-consciousness.

As I said, there are three stages of evolution—the *exoteric*, *mesoteric*, and *esoteric*; and although our individual path will take us out of the first stage and help us work through the second stage, we still have to work our way through the third and final stage to realize our divine nature.

Which brings me back to the Parable of the Good Samaritan, because to work our way through the final stage of evolution we have to transform the integrated *mesoteric* consciousness of our outer/inner self into a selfless self, and that's what mastering the art of giving love is all about…

21. The Way of All Ways

The way of Soul is the way of all ways, which is the Way; and the Way is the *life force*, which is Divine Spirit. The *life force* also creates and sustains life; ergo, *life is the Way*. This is the realization that slowly dawned upon me as I "worked" on myself with Gurdjieff's teaching and the sayings of Jesus.

Actually, I hit a brick wall with Gurdjieff's teaching—not once, but twice; and both times the omniscient guiding force of life set me free to continue my journey to my true self; otherwise I would never have awakened to the Word within and come to the astonishing realization that the Way just *Is*.

I was in my second year at university studying philosophy when I hit the brick wall the first time. I had already met Gurdjieff in a dream and asked him to take me into his inner circle of students, but I wasn't ready yet; and shortly after this dream I had an experience that changed the course of my life and opened me up to the esoteric mystery of Gurdjieff's impenetrable teaching of "work on oneself."

I drove home from university one weekend and went for a long walk down the CN railroad tracks behind our house, down to the "Little Black Bridge" (that's what we called it in my youth), and on to the manmade breakwater that connected to a little island in the middle of the Nipigon River, which created the safe little bay for our marina.

I was desperate. I sat on a rock on the island smoking one cigarette after another and pondering my future, because

WHY BOTHER?

I was beginning to have serious doubts about philosophy giving me the answers to *who am I?* And *why am I?*

I sat for hours. On my way back, I stopped and stood for a long time on the breakwater, and then I looked up into the sky and said, *"God, I know that we get nothing for nothing in this world, or any world for that matter; please tell me, what price truth?"*

The Nipigon River flowed swiftly past me where it would empty into Lake Superior, and the thought struck me that my life was like a river, and I heard myself quoting the Preacher in the book of *Ecclesiastes*: *"What profit hath a man of all his labor which he taketh under the sun? One generation passeth away, and another generation cometh; but the earth abideth forever. All the rivers run into the sea; yet the sea is not full; unto the place from whence the rivers come, thither they return again."*

Then out of the blue Sophocles' tragic play *Oedipus Rex* came to mind, and I thought of the terrible price that King Oedipus had to pay to rid Thebes of the scourge that had befallen his kingdom. Oedipus issued an edict that whoever was responsible for the plague would be banished from his kingdom, but as the tragedy would have it he learned from his blind soothsayer Tiresias that he was responsible because he had murdered his father and defiled his mother's bed; and to expiate his kingdom of the plague Oedipus gouged out his eyes and exiled himself out of his own kingdom—*and I KNEW what price truth!*

I took out my pocket notebook and wrote my *Royal Dictum*, my edict of self-exile from the kingdom of my own senses, which came to me word for word: *"I am like Oedipus Rex. I am going to exile myself out of my own kingdom. I embrace my becoming blindly, and I leave all of my sins behind me. I am going to go against the natural course of evolution, and each obstacle that I encounter I will consume."*

I felt every molecule of my being adjusting to the new reality of my *karmic destiny*, and I thanked God for the answer, and the moment I stepped off the breakwater onto the mainland I began my life of exile from the kingdom of my own senses—beginning with cigarettes. I quit smoking on the spot, took a vow of celibacy, and began my insufferable life of self-denial—*which I committed to for the rest of my life.*

That's how I broke the code of Gurdjieff's teaching of "work on oneself" and Christ's cryptic sayings and awakened to the Word within!

22. Why Do You Lie?

I had lived my *Royal Dictum,* Gurdjieff's teaching of "work on oneself," and the sayings of Jesus (not to mention dozens of aphorisms that I had collected and read to myself every morning before I began my day) for several years when I hit another brick wall and fell into another depressing state of despair.

It seemed that for all of my progress, I could not get to the headwaters of my life—to my true self; and I did not know where to turn.

I was in my bedroom one evening wallowing in despair. I was listening to Beethoven's Ninth Symphony, hoping that it would pick up my spirits, when I heard a voice in my mind ask me the question, *"Why do you lie?"*

It was a man's voice, and as clear and distinct as if he was physically in the room with me, and I started. I waited for more, but nothing else was said; but I couldn't make sense of it. I repeated the question, "Why do you lie?"

My defenses went up. "I'm a truth seeker. I don't lie." But no matter how much I tried to justify myself, I could not get that question out of my mind; and thus began the next and unbelievably difficult stage of my journey to my true self—*"working" my way through the consciousness of my false self!*

I simply had no idea how false I was until I began the acutely painful observation of my inner life; and the more I studied myself the more I saw that I lied despite myself—meaning, I lied unconsciously. But little by little, I became more and more conscious of my false self; and that's when I pulled Carl Jung, who had made a disciplined study of the unconscious, into my life—*when the student is ready, the teacher appears!*

Gurdjieff taught the concept of "false personality," but I could not quite grasp my false self until I started to answer the question, *"Why do you lie?"* As conscious as I was becoming of my false self though, it wasn't until I became acquainted with Jung's concept of the shadow that I broke into a whole new dimension of self-realization consciousness; and my journey to my true self took on such momentum that after only three and a half years I no longer needed my *Royal Dictum—honest to God, I had taken this vow for the rest of my life; that's the price I was willing to pay for truth!—* because I unexpectedly found the headwaters of my life when I experienced my own immorality one fine day in my mother's kitchen while she was kneading bread dough on the kitchen table!

23. To Thine Own Self Be True

"This above all: to thine own self be true, and it must follow as the night the day, thou canst not then be false to any man," said Polonius to his son Laertes, who was sailing to France in Shakespeare's play *Hamlet*; but which self?

This was my dilemma; but I did not know it was my dilemma because I thought that I was true to myself until I heard the question, *"Why do you lie?"* It took a few years of obsessive self-observation to see that I was an unconscious liar, and I dedicated every ounce of energy that I could spare to stop lying.

I became so pathologically committed to being honest in my thoughts words and deeds that I experienced an actual shift in consciousness one evening while I was waiting on tables at the Nipigon Inn Hotel.

I was working three jobs that summer: construction work during the day helping the bricklayers who were building the new police station in Nipigon, taking the census for the federal government for a few hours after working my day job, and waiting on tables in the Nipigon Inn Hotel in the evenings; and it was while waiting on tables one evening that I experienced my dramatic shift in consciousness.

I had exiled myself out of the kingdom of sensual pleasure with my *Royal Dictum*, but the female strippers that were performing on stage all evening aroused me sexually and it took all I had to *non-identify* with the desire that they aroused.

Non-identification was one of Gurdjieff's techniques for "working" on oneself, which was next to impossible to master; but because I had broken the code of this esoteric technique for transforming one's consciousness with my *Royal Dictum,* I could *non-identify* with anything; and all evening long I *non-identified* with the strippers.

In effect, I detached from any sexual emotions that the stripers aroused in me; and I also *non-identified* with the terrible summer cold that I had. This technique of *non-identification* had created in me a state of consciousness where I was indifferent to life, a state of consciousness that was neither for nor against life—which helped me to see the esoteric meaning of Christ's perplexing saying, **"But let your communication be, Yea yea; Nay nay; for whatsoever is more than these cometh of evil"** (Math. 5: 37). I called this incredible neither/nor state of consciousness my "sanctuary." In the Sufi sense, I had learned how to be "in the world but not of the world."

The naked strippers were unbelievable seductive, and it took all I had to *non-identify* with them, and my wicked summer cold made working very hard; but I refused to give in, and I resisted the temptation all night long—and then it happened.

I felt a "snap" inside me. I actually felt something "snap," and I felt an immediate shift in consciousness from the "prison" of one part of myself to the "freedom" of another part of myself, and I KNEW that I was free of the hold my false self had on me!

I didn't know what had just happened, but I could not deny the actual "snap" that sprung me free me from myself; but a few days later I recalled that one of Gurdjieff's students had exactly the same experience while "working" on himself.

A. R. Orage, the celebrated literary critic from England, had taken up Gurjdieff's Work and was living at Gurdjieff's Institute for the Harmonious Development of Man at the Priory in Fontainebleau, France. Gurdjieff was a merciless taskmaster, and he had his students do all kinds of work that they never dreamt of doing, but it was all designed to transform their consciousness and create what he called a "Work self," and he had Orage dig a ditch for no apparent reason.

Orage couldn't see the logic of this senseless task, but he dug and dug and dug and *non-identified* with his digging until he felt a "snap" inside, and he knew that he had made an enormous breakthrough; and he finally understood why Gurdjieff pushed his students the way he did. He finally saw the sanity of Gurdieff's "insanity"!

Orage experienced the same freedom that I experienced, and from that moment on I no longer felt trapped by my own falseness. I had shifted my center of gravity from the false self of my *non-being* to the authentic self of my *being,* and that's when I came to the astonishing realization that **no matter how true one is to himself, if it is his false self that he is being true to his whole life is a lie!**

I finally answered the question, *"why do you lie?"* I lied because my center of gravity—the "I" of my personality—was fixed in my false self, and everything that I said and did was *ipso facto* inauthentic; and from the moment I felt that "snap" I could always tell a lie from the truth in myself, which gave me uncanny insight into the shadow side of life—which I finally wrote about last year in the second volume of my spiritual musings, *Old Whore Life: Exploring the Shadow Side of Karma.*

24. The Agnostic Christian

After I shifted my center of gravity from my inauthentic self to my authentic self that night waiting on tables in the Nipigon Inn Hotel while the strippers from Montreal gyrated their naked bodies on stage, I discerned the psycho/spiritual meaning of the philosophical concepts of *being* and *non-being*, and Sartre's philosophy opened up to me; and when he spoke of *mauvaise foi* (bad faith), I knew exactly what he was talking about—because this spoke to one's false self, regardless if one was aware of his false self or not, like the United Church minister I met one beautiful summer morning in my hometown.

I was painting the exterior of the Roman Catholic priest's residence, and in the afternoon of my second day I noticed that they were moving boxes into the United Church manse next door. Around nine o'clock the next morning the new minister stepped out the back door of the manse with a cup of coffee in his hands. He didn't notice me right away, but I watched him taking in his new surroundings. I could sense his thoughts: *I wonder what my life in this town is going to be like?*

He was not as young as I expected for a new minister. In fact, he looked like he was ready for retirement, which I learned later he was; he was just filling in until there was a minister available for the Nipigon parish. "Good morning," I said, from my side of the fence. I was standing on my ladder painting the eaves.

Surprised, he turned to me. "Yes, it is a good morning."

"Are you the new minister?" I asked.

"Well, yes and no. I'm just filling in until we find someone."

"Yeah, there's a shortage these days, isn't there?" I said, deliberately; I was hoping to open up a dialogue on the question of gay ministers, which was the burning issue of the day for the United Church.

"Yes, we could sure use some new recruits," he replied.

"You've got a whole flank waiting to be ordained," I responded.

"What do you mean?" he asked.

"Isn't this what the whole issue of gay ministers is about in your church?"

"Oh, I see where you're coming from. And where do you stand on the issue?" he asked, walking up to the fence for a more intimate conversation.

I adjusted my position on the ladder to face him, "I have no issue with gay ministers. I do have issues with unmarried priests, though. I think it's damn near impossible to suppress the natural urges of one's libido. I don't think Jesus would mind if his vicars were married. He probably was."

"Oh," the interim minister replied. "Why do you say that?"

"That's what the rumor is," I said, with an ironic smile. I had just read the fascinating book *The Holy Blood and the Holy Grail,* which contended that Jesus did not die on the cross and that he went on to marry Mary Magdalene and sired a family—which years later inspired the controversial movie *The DaVinci Code,* based on Dan Brown's novel that was condemned by the Vatican.

WHY BOTHER?

This opened up our dialogue, and before long he revealed that he no longer believed that Jesus was the Son of God, making some oblique reference to the Grand Inquisitor in Dostoevsky's novel *The Brothers Karamazov*, but he couldn't speak about that openly with his parishioners because he didn't want to rob them of their faith.

"But isn't that the whole premise of Christianity, that God sacrificed his only begotten Son on the cross to wash away the sins of the world?" I asked.

"That's all myth," he replied.

"How long have you held this belief?" I asked.

"A long time. Maybe twenty years," he said. "I'm what you might call an agnostic Christian."

"*Agnostic Christian?*" I repeated. "That's an oxymoron."

I felt him instantly go on the defensive. "Why do you say that?"

"A Christian is by definition someone who gets to know God through his Son Jesus Christ, and an agnostic is someone who by definition cannot know God; that's why I find it oxymoronic to be both a Christian and an agnostic."

"You're not just a housepainter, are you?" he said, thrown off balance.

"I have to do something to support my literary aspirations," I said.

"Oh, I see," he said; but our little dialectic quickly faded into small talk, and before long he excused himself so I could get back to work; but I couldn't help but smile to myself all day long at the man's *mauvaise foi*.

25. An Honest Persuasion

In his book *Crossing the Unknown Sea, Work as a Pilgrimage of Identity*, David Whyte gives us a poetic insight into the transformative nature of work that speaks to the riddle of the Good Samaritan:

"All our great artists and religious traditions take equally great pains to inform us that we must never mistake a good *career* for good work. Life is a creative, intimate and unpredictable conversation if it is nothing else, spoken or unspoken, and our *life* and our *work* are both the result of the particular way we hold that passionate conversation." (Chapter 1, *Courage and Conversation: Setting Out with a Firm Persuasion*)

The agnostic Christian minister lacked a *firm persuasion*, and his life was a lie; but he didn't want to acknowledge it. It would threaten his livelihood if he had the courage of his convictions. He wasn't willing to be bought with a price, as St. Paul would say, and he would never step into the *mesoteric* circle of evolution.

When I came back from France I got a job selling an intangible. It was a university scholarship trust fund called University Scholarships of Canada; but this job began to have a very strange effect upon me.

I was a very affable, articulate, curly haired good looking young man and I was getting good at selling this intangible, but I began to notice that I was not selling the product, as such; I was selling myself. I was familiar with

WHY BOTHER?

Arthur Miller's play *Death of a Salesman,* and I began to panic.

Willy Loman is a salesman in Miller's play, and along his life's path he slowly compromises himself away, which made him an unfulfilled and unhappy man, and I didn't want to become like Willy Loman (who ends up committing suicide so his son could collect his life insurance policy to help finance his business venture); so I quit my job.

My next job came after I dropped out of university. I started my own contract painting business, and I did everything in my power to be honest in my work. As David Whyte would say, I did my work with a *firm persuasion*.

Because life *is* the Way, the way we live our life (the values we live by) engages us in a very personal, intimate *conversation* with life; and if we do not have an *honest conversation* with a *firm persuasion* we will suffer the same fate as the agnostic Christian minister and the tragic salesman Willy Loman.

I didn't articulate it in these terms at the time, but the question I asked myself when I was selling this intangible was, "what difference does it make how I make my sale, as long as I make it?" But I began to feel the difference.

It didn't matter how much I believed in the product I was selling, I no longer wanted to put myself in a position where I might compromise myself just to make my sale—because I couldn't trust myself; and I had to quit.

I could have stayed and worked through my moral dilemma, but I chose to move on; and I enrolled at university as an adult student to study philosophy.

26. As Flies to Wanton Boys

I was born *mesoterically minded*, which means that I was ready to take evolution into my own hands; that's why I could not stick to one path to find my true self. But whatever path we take in life, our work becomes our way; and if we don't engage in our work with an *honest persuasion* we obligate ourselves to life.

And the more obligated we are to life, the more we suffer the capricious winds of our own karmic fate. The Duke of Gloucester in Shakespeare's *King Lear* was too arrogant to see his own folly, and when misfortune befalls him he shouts, *"As flies to wanton boys are we to the gods, they kill us for their sport."* And so do we all blame the gods for our misfortunes until life wakes us up to our own folly.

It cost me thirty thousand dollars—and so much emotional distress that I became an insomniac—to learn how karma really works. I was foolish to take on a contract that I couldn't handle, and I paid a very dear price for my folly.

I got a contract from a Thunder Bay contractor to hang the drywall, tape, and paint seven new houses on the native reservation in my hometown of Nipigon, but I wasn't knowledgeable enough about hanging and taping drywall to do this job justice, and my contract went so sour on me that it affected my health, and bank account.

I could have blamed the four or five native workers that worked for me (I was obligated to hire men from the reserve for this contract) who just dropped their tools when

WHY BOTHER?

moose hunting season came along and didn't show up for two weeks when I was working under a deadline (it cost me one hundred dollars a day over the deadline), and I could have blamed the general contractor for his mismanagement of the job by putting an inexperienced young man in charge of the whole project; but I couldn't.

It was *my* contract, and *my* responsibility; so when my inexperienced drywall hangers hung the drywall with all kinds of deficiencies for the taper to fix, it was *my* responsibility to correct them; and when the inexperienced tapers left all kinds of deficiencies for the painters to correct, it was *my* responsibility to correct them; and when the inexperienced painters left all kinds of deficiencies, it was *my* responsibility to correct them—because it was *my* contract, and I was obligated to meet the standards of excellence demanded by the building inspector who made my life a living hell; and what I thought was going to be a sweet contract turned out to be a bitter nightmare.

Instead of making twenty thousand dollars as I anticipated, I lost thirty thousand dollars; but as distressing as this job turned out to be, the price that I paid woke me up to my own folly and initiated me into the *mesoteric* mystery of karmic accountability!

27. Bought With a Price

When we take evolution into our own hands we have to take karmic responsibility for our life. We cannot blame the gods for what happens to us. *"The fault, dear Brutus, lies not in our stars, but in ourselves if we are underlings,"* said Shakespeare in *Julius Caesar*; this is what it means to have an *honest conversation* with life.

The Samaritan had an *honest conversation* with life. When he stopped to help the injured man by the side of the road he did so out of a *firm persuasion* that it was the right thing to do, and he did it because he was true to his honest self. He was willing to pay the "price" to put himself out for the injured man.

The priest, whom one would expect to help the injured man because a priest by definition should be righteous and obey the commandments of God, did not stop to help because it would have cost him; and the Levite walked on by also because it would have cost him; but what is this "price" that the priest and Levite did not want to pay?

In his first letter to the Corinthians St. Paul draws the distinction between the *exoteric* and *mesoteric* circles of life. In the *exoteric* circle, we are servants of men; and in the *mesoteric* circle we are servants of the Way (St. Paul uses the word Christ for Way):

"Let every man abide in the same calling wherein he was called. Art thou called being a servant? care not for it: but if thou mayest be made free, use it rather. For he that is called in the Lord, being a servant, is the Lord's freeman:

WHY BOTHER?

likewise also he that is called, being free is Christ's servant. Ye are bought with a price; be not ye the servants of men" (I Cor. 7: 20-23).

When St. Paul says *"let every man abide in the same calling wherein he was called,"* he is saying that the work one is called to do (his job, profession, or career) is his way, or personal path through life, and that he must *abide* (be true, or have an *honest persuasion)* to his path; and if one is called by his work to compromise himself (*art thou called being a servant?),* he must not yield himself (*care not for it*), unless in the yielding *he is made free*—which simply means that one has yielded without compromising his integrity; but if one is *called in the Lord* (called to live the *mesoteric* life of the Way), he is a servant of Christ (the Way) and yields freedom in his service to Christ (the Way); and the "price" that it costs to become the *Lord's freeman* (one's true self) is to not compromise oneself to life (*be not ye servants of men*); meaning, live life with a *firm persuasion.*

St. Paul is very cryptic about taking evolution into our own hands, but he's saying that if we use life for selfish ends we will not pay our karmic debt to life, and we will not realize our spiritual freedom; so the "price" that the priest and Levite did not want to pay to help the injured man was their own selfish nature.

They weren't willing to freely give of themselves, because they weren't ready yet to sacrifice the consciousness of their mortal human self for *eternal life.* That's what Jesus meant when he said, **"He that loveth his life shall lose it; and he that hateth his life in this world shall keep unto life eternal"** (John 12: 25).

When we are called by life to pay the "price" then, we are called to forfeit that selfish part of ourselves that keeps us out of the *kingdom of God* and *eternal life*.

28. On the Way to Jericho

"Life is a journey of the self," said St. Padre Pio, but from where does the self come and where is the self going? Or, as the artist Paul Gauguin expressed it in his famous masterpiece: Where do we come from? What are we? Where are we going?

I answered these three questions, which is why Carl Jung came to me in a dream one night to talk about my book *The Way of Soul*. He wanted to know about "the alpha and omega of the self"—meaning, the beginning and end of the self.

The self comes from the Body of God as a soul seed, and it evolves through the life process to create its own reflective self-consciousness, or as John Keats discerned, its own identity—*"a bliss peculiar to each one by individual existence."*

This "bliss" is a new "I" of God, and this new "I" of God has to evolve until it becomes conscious of its divine nature. This is the purpose of life.

Jesus came into the world to help us find our way to God-realization consciousness, which he called *kingdom of God*. Jesus said: **"Except a man be born again, he cannot see the kingdom of God"** (John 3: 3). This is a deep mystery:

"Nichodemus said unto him, how can a man be born when he is old? Can he enter a second time into his mother's womb, and be born?

Jesus answered, ***Verily, verily, I say unto thee, Except a man be born of water and of the Spirit, he cannot enter into the kingdom of God. That which is born of the flesh is flesh; and that which is born of the Spirit is spirit***" (John 3: 4-6).

As I experienced in my first human lifetime, our reflective self is born of the life process; hence, it is born of the flesh—meaning, it is born of the material consciousness of life; but because the consciousness of life is both material and spiritual, our reflective self-consciousness is both material and spiritual in nature. This is why St. Paul called our reflective self a "selfsame thing." And liberating our spiritual self from our material self is what spiritual rebirth is all about, but it is not easy:

"For godly sorrow worketh repentance unto salvation not to be repented of; but the sorrow of the world worketh death. For behold this selfsame thing, that ye sorrowed after a godly sort, what carefulness it wrought in you, yea, what clearing of yourselves, yea, what indignation, yea, what fear, yea, what vehement desire, yea, what zeal, yea, what revenge" (11 Cor. 7: 10-11).

Again, Paul is very cryptic about taking evolution into our own hands (which is the *mesoteric* process of being born again); but by *godly sorrow* he meant the special effort one makes to transform the consciousness of his lower self (as I did that night in the bar when I *non-identified* with the strippers). With this kind of special effort, one transforms the consciousness of his lower self and realizes *salvation not to be repented of*—meaning, the energy of *eternal life*;

which simply means that one spiritualizes the consciousness of his lower self and makes the two selves into one soul self.

St. Paul draws a distinction between the two kinds of suffering. In one kind of suffering, which he called the *sorrow of the world*, one does not spiritualize the consciousness of his lower self; hence, *the sorrow of the world worketh death;* but when one learns the secret of how to spiritualize the energy of one's suffering (Jesus called it storing one's "treasures in heaven"), one will work *repentance unto salvation not to be repented of*—meaning, *eternal life,* or God-realization consciousness. *Repentance* is St. Paul's word for spiritual energy. St. Padre Pio called this special energy his "glory." Jesus called it "treasures in heaven," and I called it *virtue*.

Being born again then is a process. It doesn't just happen. It takes time to transform the consciousness of our lower self; and when one has spiritualized his lower self enough he will experience a shift in consciousness from his lower self to his higher self, as I did in my mother's kitchen that summer day while she was kneading bread dough.

We are all on the way to Jericho, then; and by this I mean that Jesus reflects the spiritual message of the Way (being born again) in his parable of the Good Samaritan, because by stopping to help the injured man on his way to Jericho the Samaritan was spiritualizing the consciousness of his lower self by making a special effort *(godly sorrow)* to nurse the injured man's wounds and pay an innkeeper to look after him.

The Samaritan showed mercy for the injured man, and by his helpful efforts he did the injured man good, and the good that he did earned him the special energy that I came to identify as *virtue*; and one day the Good Samaritan would realize enough *virtue* to be born again. That's why Jesus said to the cynical lawyer, **"Go out and do likewise,"** because that was how he could earn *eternal life*.

29. The Selfsame Thing

I would not have solved the mystery of "the alpha and omega of the self" had I not had seven past-life regressions. I can only attribute it to providential design (my regressionist and I had no idea this was going to happen), but in my fourth regression I found myself going all the way back to where I came from, the Body of God, the Great Ocean of Love and Mercy; but I only had Soul consciousness, not self-consciousness.

Once I experienced myself in the pure bliss of God's Body, I found myself in my first primordial human lifetime where I experienced the actual dawning of my reflective self-consciousness. It was a very dim, rudimentary sense of self, but I was aware of myself for the first time in my life, and I was totally baffled by my sense of self-awareness.

As I've already said, I was the alpha male of a clan of ten or twelve members, and I controlled them with brute force. I grunted all the time to show my authority, and I savagely beat any member who showed the least defiance; but I noticed that whenever they cowered in fear every time I gave one of my power grunts they forfeited their will to me, and I realized this was how I appropriated their *life force* and individuated my sense of self.

As an observer of my own experience, I caught my second glimpse into the Divine Plan of God. My first glimpse was experiencing myself as an atom in the Body of God. As Keats discerned, I was an *atom of perception* without self-consciousness; but then I found myself in my primordial lifetime where I experienced the birth of my reflective self-consciousness, and the puzzle of my existence began to make sense.

Now that I had a reflective self, with each new life that I lived I grew in my sense of self—or, as Keats would say, I began to *acquire an identity*. And the more identity that I acquired with each new life, the more I became *personally myself*.

After hundreds or perhaps thousands of lifetimes, I acquired enough *personal identity* to realize that there had to be more to life than what I was experiencing; and that's when I began to look for answers to the mystery of life—which brought me to my lifetime as Phaedrus in ancient Greece where I sought out Pythagoras because I had heard whispers and rumors in Athens that he possessed a secret knowledge of the Soul.

I learned about my Greek lifetime in another regression. I was born into a wealthy aristocratic family and was being groomed for politics, but something was missing in my life. I wanted to know the mystery of life. I could see that behind the perishable nature of life there was something that did not die, and I wanted to know if Pythagoras could tell me what this imperishable quality was, so I sailed to Italy to seek him out. He accepted me into his mystery school, and I began to live the secret teaching of the Way.

Carl Jung also felt as I did in my lifetime as Phaedrus. In the Prologue to his autobiography *Memories, Dreams, Reflections* he writes: "Life has always seemed to me like a plant that lives on its rhizome. Its true life is invisible, hidden in the rhizome. The part that appears above ground lasts only a single summer. Then it withers away—an ephemeral apparition. When we think of the unending growth and decay of life and civilizations, we cannot escape the impression of absolute nullity. Yet I have never lost a sense of something that lives and endures underneath the eternal flux. What we see is the blossom, which passes. The rhizome remains."

This is why he came to me in a dream to talk about *the way of Soul* that I first learned from Pythagoras. Pythagoras taught that we create a new personality with each life we live, but it does not die when our body dies. Each personality that we create with every new life that we live individuates our *personal identity,* or what Jung called the Self—the central archetype of our life; which means that our personality is not our real self. Our personality is the means by which our real imperishable self acquires identity—*"a bliss peculiar to each one by individual existence,"* as Keats so poetically expressed it.

This is what St. Paul meant by *selfsame thing.* He was referring to the outer self of our personality and the individuating consciousness of our "incorruptible" inner soul self; and his teaching, which he learned from the Essenes after his life-changing encounter with the spirit of Jesus Christ on the road to Damascus, was all about liberating the inner self from the outer self—what Jesus referred to as being born again:

"So when this corruptible shall have put on incorruption, and this mortal shall have put on immortality, then shall be brought to pass the saying that is written, Death is swallowed up in victory. O death, where is thy sting? O grave, where is thy victory? The sting of death is sin; and the strength of sin is the law" (I Cor. 15: 54-56).

By *sin*, St. Paul meant the karma that the outer self creates that keeps soul bound to the recurring cycle of life and death; and by *law*, he meant the secret teaching of *the way of Christ* that wakes one up to *sin* and spiritualizes the ephemeral consciousness of his outer self—hence, immortalizing the self. *This mortal shall have put on immortality*, as St. Paul cryptically expressed the birth of one's spiritual self.

In a word, we have a dual consciousness. We have an outer self, which is the ephemeral personality that we create with each life we live, and we have an eternal inner self that grows in self-identity with each new personality that we create; but it is not ours to keep. We belong to life because life created us through the evolutionary process of karma and reincarnation, and the only way to break the endless cycle of life and death is to pay life back for all the energy that it took to create our individual identity.

This is why Jesus told the Parable of the Good Samaritan to the cynical lawyer. Couching the secret teaching of spiritual rebirth in his parable, Jesus told him that if he wanted *eternal life* he would have to start paying life back for his own life; and he could do that by having compassion for his neighbor. In effect, Jesus was saying, *the only way you will enter the kingdom of God is to love your fellow man.*

30. The Soul's Real Code

According to James Hillman, a Jungian analyst and author of *The Soul's Code, In Search of Character and Calling*, "each person bears a uniqueness that asks to be lived and that is already present before it can be lived." This is the soul's code, which he calls "the acorn theory," but because we are free to choose our own *karmic destiny* we seem to be forever in conflict with our soul's code—hence, the inevitable conclusion that was forced upon me by the logic of my own spiritual quest: *we have to align our two destinies!*

As I said in my novel *What Would I Say Today If I Were To Die Tomorrow?* — "We live more than one life, and it is foolish to deny this simply truth," which adds a whole new dimension to Hillman's acorn theory that has to be taken into consideration to make sense of our soul's code.

Psychologists, however brilliant (Jung will fascinate me till the day I die), will never make sense of the soul's code until they come to the realization that the only way to realize our *spiritual destiny* (soul's spiritual code) is through our *karmic destiny* (soul's personal, or daemonic code); and by *spiritual destiny* I mean our pre-scripted destiny to become God-realized Souls, and by *karmic destiny* I mean our own individual code that arises out of all our past lives—like Mozart's destiny, Lincoln's destiny, Shakespeare's destiny, Einstein's destiny, Gandhi's destiny, and so on.

No two souls create the same karma, so no two souls will have the same *karmic destiny*—which is why the Sufis say that there are as many ways to God as there are souls of man; and with each life we live we grow and evolve in our own karmic path, until one day our path calls us to align our *karmic destiny* with our *spiritual destiny*.

When our path calls, we have to heed the call; otherwise we will suffer. Countless souls have gone to their grave miserable and unfulfilled because they did not heed the call of their personal path, or *karmic destiny*. I fought the call to my path, and I suffered; but Providence mercifully intervened (as it does with every soul that is ready to enter the *mesoteric* stage of evolution) and severed me from my life's course and set me on a new path that would bring my *karmic destiny* into alignment with my *spiritual destiny*:

At the age of twenty one I took over a pool hall business in my hometown, which I expanded to include a pin ball and cigarette vending machine business, and I could have become a successful businessman (I believe I did the first time I lived my same life), but I became "possessed" one night in my second year of business (which I now believe to be the personality of my past lifetime as *le salaud de Paris*) and had a sexual experience that so shocked my conscience that I vowed to find out why I did what I did or die trying, because I knew that the person who did what he did wasn't me; or, rather (and this is the mystery of my quest), it was me, but it wasn't me; it was my karmic shadow self that took the best energies of my life to resolve and integrate with my true self.

I sold my business and went to France to begin my quest for my true self, because the person who did what he did that night wasn't the real me; thus began years of seeking for a teaching that would explain my life. That's how I pulled Gurdjieff into my life—because his teaching of "work on oneself" was precisely the teaching that I needed to begin the transformation of my karmic shadow self!

My karmic shadow self was the dark, repressed side of all my past-life personalities, and it doesn't matter how hard one tries to repress it, it will one day come out to possess you—because it cries to be resolved!

Why? Why does the shadow want to be resolved? Did Mr. Hyde want Dr. Jekyll to resolve him? One wouldn't think so the way Mr. Hyde behaved. And yet in the end, Dr. Jekyll wanted to resolve Mr. Hyde. And herein lies the mystery of the self!

Mr. Hyde is Dr. Jekyll's dark side; ergo, he is no less a part of Dr. Jekyll's self-consciousness than his everyday visible personality. Which means that the individuating consciousness of Dr. Jekyll's soul includes both selves; and since Dr. Jekyll's soul is teleologically driven to become God-realized, one can understand why the shadow side of one's personality cries out to be resolved—because soul is divinely ordained to resolve itself. This is why I experienced what I did that night that shocked my conscience awake—the sexual experience that brutally shocked my conscience awake was my soul's cry to be resolved just as Mr. Hyde possessing Dr. Jekyll's personality!

But in France I had another experience that so complicated my quest for my true self that I thought I would lose my mind again like I did in my past lifetime as Salam the Sufi in 15th Century Persia when I failed to tame my "tiger of desire"—I accidentally awakened the "serpent fire" one night while meditating on a maple leaf, and it took me

years of relentless effort to harness the kundalini energy and tame my "tiger of desire"!
    Mine was not an easy path…

31. A Jungian Slip

We all know what a *Freudian slip* is, but who ever heard of a *Jungian slip*?

A *Freudian slip* speaks to the personal level of the unconscious, what one really feels or thinks about someone or something that just slips out of one's mouth when one tries to conceal his real thoughts or feelings; for example, when giving his condolences to a friend's wife at her abusive, miserable husband's funeral, instead of saying, "I'm so sorry," the friend unconsciously says, "Congratulations—"

Whereas a *Jungian slip* speaks to one's soul, the deepest level of the unconscious, what one knows he should be doing to realize his soul's code, like the experience David Whyte had one day that called him to hazard and altered the course of his life.

I spotted this *Jungian slip* in Whyte's book *Crossing the Unknown Sea*, which Whyte also recognized upon reflection after his slip of the tongue but didn't call it a *Jungian slip* because this term didn't exist until I made it up while writing this book to identify how our soul cries out to us to step onto the path that we are destined to live to realize our soul's code. Here's the context of David Whyte's *Jungian slip*:

David Whyte was called to poetry at an early age, but the stark reality of life's demands for survival always kept him from stepping onto his destined path to devote his life to the path of poetry—which would bring his *karmic destiny* into alignment with his pre-scripted *spiritual destiny* and integrate his outer and inner self. So he chose marine biology for his career because it offered a much better opportunity to make a living than writing poetry; but as hard as he tried, he couldn't silence the cry of his soul to be a poet.

He graduated and was fortunate to land an ideal job as a naturalist in the Galapagos Islands which he loved but had to leave after a few years because destiny called; and ten years after Galapagos he got a position on a wooded island in the Pacific Northwest USA for a nonprofit institution that kept him so busy that he all but silenced his soul's cry to step onto his destined path of poetry—until the day of his *Jungian slip,* that is:

"One morning, hurtling from my desk toward the photocopier, I passed a roomful of my colleagues just about to start a meeting. There was someone I needed to talk to. I saw immediately that he wasn't among them, but I put my head in the door before they could begin, and in a very loud, urgent voice, I said, 'Has anyone seen David?'" (*Crossing the Unknown Sea, Work as a Pilgrimage of Identity,* by David Whyte)

After a stunned silence, everyone started to laugh—because David Whyte happened to be the only David who worked there! In that moment of stark realization, David realized that he had become a stranger to himself. In effect, he had lost his way. And that's when the merciful grace of the omniscient guiding force of life provided him with the opportunity to step onto the path that he was destined to live—writing poetry.

WHY BOTHER?

David had a timely conversation (*talk about meaningful coincidence!*) with his friend and monk Brother David that night, and over a glass of cabernet they read a poem by Rilke, Brother David reading it in his German text and David Whyte following in his English text, and the symbol of the swan in the poem spoke to David's call to *karmic destiny* and moved him to shift his priorities—he had to let go of his old life and take up his new life of poetry as Rilke's poem called for: *"And to die, which is the letting go/of the ground we stand on and cling to every day."*

"Has anyone seen David?" was his *Jungian slip*. It was his *soul's desperate cry to individuation*—which meant that he was called to step into the *mesoteric* circle of life and take evolution into his own hands, because the *exoteric* circle of life could no longer nourish his hungry soul. As much as he tried to deny his *karmic destiny*, he could not; and neither could the celebrated Canadian artist Robert Bateman. He too made a *Jungian slip*.

Robert Bateman was also called early to the path of art. It was his *karmic destiny*, and for years he painted abstract art because this was what artists painted at the time. One day however he finished a painting and stood it up against a wall and studied it for a while, and then he heard himself asking, *"Is that it? Is that all there is to art?"*

That was his *Jungian slip*. That was his soul's desperate cry to leave the path of abstract expressionism and move on to something else; but what?

Again, by the merciful grace of the omniscient guiding force of life he was nudged to go across the border to take in a viewing of the American artist Andrew Wyeth's work in Buffalo NY, and when he studied the realist painter's art Bateman had what he called his road to

Damascus experience and exclaimed to himself, *"I found my way!"*

He went back to his roots and started painting nature, and the more he painted nature the more he aligned his *karmic destiny* with his *spiritual destiny* and grew in what Jung called in his wholeness and singleness of self.

And the mystical artist Jerry Wennstrom also had his *Jungian slip* which he unconsciously revealed when he unexpectedly advised his artist friend Gilbert to gracefully accept the changes he had to make because of his failing eyesight:

"Gilbert, your life is in God's hands. If you can no longer paint or do your art, why don't you just let go of it. Trust what is happening to you. You will always be creative. Even if you die, that will be creative." (*The Inspired Heart*, by Jerry Wennstrom)

Little did Jerry Wennstrom realize that his soul was crying out for him to die to his own artistic process because it had brought him as far as he could go with it and he had to sacrifice his god of art to find a new path to wholeness; and not long after his *Jungian slip* Jerry began to feel the oppressive weight of his spiritual dilemma: "Art began to feel like a trap to me, yet I was afraid to let go of it. After much praying for guidance, I was finally able to destroy what I had created."

Jerry had the courage to listen to his *soul's desperate cry for individuation* and stepped into the *mesoteric* circle of life by burning all of his art and giving away his possessions and surrendering his life to the Moment; and for fifteen years he lived the mystical life of a man whose destiny was

WHY BOTHER?

in God's hands until his *karmic destiny* merged with his *spiritual destiny* to forge a new path by making art and his life one path.

Like Jerry Wennstrom, the poet David Whyte, and the artist Robert Bateman, who all love doing what they do today, so too did the lawyer in the parable of the Good Samaritan make a *Jungian slip* when he asked Jesus, *"What shall I do to inherit eternal life?"*

Despite the cynicism, this was his *soul's cry for individuation,* and the merciful omniscient guiding force of life in the person of Jesus Christ opened the door for him with the Parable of the Good Samaritan to help step into the *mesoteric* circle of life—which Jesus called the *kingdom of heaven*!

32. The Kingdom of Heaven

Not everyone is ready for the *kingdom of heaven*. It takes many lifetimes to grow enough in self-realization consciousness to create a *karmic destiny* that will align one's life with one's *spiritual destiny* to realize wholeness and singleness of self.

Social scientists would like to believe in the ten thousand hour theory—that it takes ten thousand hours to cultivate the genius of one's talent; but the truth is that it takes many lifetimes to evolve an individual genius like Whyte's, Bateman's, or Wennstrom's—not to mention the monumental genius of men like Mozart, Da Vinci, and Einstein. This is the wisdom that Jesus couched in the *Parable of the Laborers in the Vineyard*:

For the kingdom of heaven is like unto a man that is an householder which went out early in the morning to hire laborers in his vineyard. And when he had agreed with the laborers for a penny a day, he sent them into his vineyard. And he went about the third hour, and saw others standing idle in the marketplace. And said unto them; Go ye also into the vineyard, and whatsoever is right I will give you. And they went their way. Again he went about the sixth and ninth hour, and did likewise. And about the eleventh hour he went out, and found others standing idle, and saith unto them, Why stand ye here all day idle? They say unto him, Because no man hath hired us. He saith unto them, Go ye also into the vineyard; and whatsoever is right, that shall ye receive. So when even was

WHY BOTHER?

come, the lord of the vineyard saith unto the steward, Call the laborers, and give them their hire, beginning from the last unto the first. And when they came that were hired about the eleventh hour, they received every man a penny. But when the first came, they supposed that they should have received more; and they likewise received every man a penny. And when they had received it, they murmured against the goodman of the house. Saying, These last have wrought but one hour, and thou hast made them equal unto us, which have borne the burden and heat of the day. But he answered one of them, and said, Friend, I do thee no wrong: didst thou not agree with me for a penny? Take that thine is, and go thy way. I will give unto this last, even as unto thee. Is it not lawful for me to do what I will with mine own? Is thine eye evil, because I am good? So the last shall be first, and the first last; for many be called, but few chosen. (Math. 8: 1-16)

The *kingdom of heaven* is not a place, as such; it is an esoteric process of self-transformation, and a state of higher consciousness. The *kingdom of heaven* is the *mesoteric* circle of life, the second stage of evolution where one makes conscious effort to align his *karmic destiny* with his *spiritual destiny* and become one whole, single self.

In the *exoteric* circle of life soul is unaware of the karmic process of evolution, and from lifetime to lifetime it will evolve its own *karmic destiny* by the choices it makes. For example, somewhere along the way a person may take an interest in music, which he will bring into his next life; and he expands upon his innate musical interest, and in another life he does the same, and so on creating his *soul's karmic code* until in one life he is born with a musical talent ready to explode into the world—like Wolfgang Amadeus Mozart.

A person's *karmic destiny* is his or her individual genius, the evolved talent of many lifetimes; and as one lives their *karmic destiny* (whether they take one thousand hours or ten thousand hours to bring it to the fore in their life) they integrate the consciousness of their outer karmic self with their inner spiritual self and become one self:

"For when the master himself was asked by someone when the kingdom would come, he said, **'When the two will be one, and the outer like the inner, and the male with the female, neither male nor female.'**" (Marvin Meyer's *The Unknown Sayings of Jesus*)

In the deepest, most Jungian sense of the term, *kingdom of heaven* is the conscious individuation of the self of man that comes to fruition when the two selves become one self; but the individuation of the self does not stop there. The self continues to grow in the *mesoteric* circle of life until it is ready to enter the third and final stage of evolution, which is the *esoteric* stage of transforming the self into a selfless self—a God-realized Soul.

In the *Parable of the Laborers in the Vineyard*, Jesus calls all those souls in the *exoteric* circle of life that are willing to come to the vineyard (*mesoteric* stage of evolution) to work, and the price agreed upon is one penny, which is Christ's symbolic way of saying that the laborers will all be rewarded according to their own *individuation process*—meaning, they will receive one penny for whatever state of individuation they realize.

WHY BOTHER?

The disgruntlement that some of the laborers who worked much longer than others who came into the vineyard later in the day speaks to their own level of individuation, which means that they have more work to do on themselves to become one self.

"Take that thine is, and go thy way," said Jesus to these disgruntled laborers. ***"I will give unto this last, even as unto thee. Is it not lawful for me to do what I will with mine own? Is thine eye evil, because I am good? So the last shall be first, and the first last; for many be called, but few chosen."***

Jesus is the *lord of the vineyard,* and the laborers are the men he has called to work in his *vineyard*—meaning that they were called to do the secret work of *making the two selves one* (the first will be the same as the last), but at the end of the day some of the laborers were given their due and told to go their way because they were not yet ready to make one self out of two. In Christ's words, they were called but not chosen.

33. Keepers of the Flame

When one is called to his *karmic destiny*, he is called to become a *Keeper of the Flame*—which is the individuated consciousness of his *soul's karmic code*, like David Whyte who was called to share his *conversation* with life in his poetry.

"To be human /is to become visible /while carrying /what is hidden /as a gift to others," says Whyte in his poem *What to Remember when Waking*. Awake now to his calling, he is bringing his *hidden gift* to the world with his poetry and public talks, and in doing so he has become a *Keeper of the Holy Flame of God*.

"Poetry is an act of the imagination that transforms reality into a deeper perception of what is," said the American poet Adrienne Rich, another *Keeper of the Flame* who opens our window on life with her poetry; and in doing so, in her own individual way (which Whyte calls *conversation* with life) helps us to make sense of the human condition.

A *Keeper of the Flame* is someone who shares their individual genius with the world, because they have to. They have no choice, as David Whyte tells us in his book *Crossing the Unknown Sea*. "Has anyone seen David?" his soul asked, and David stepped into the *vineyard* of the Way to live his *karmic destiny* of becoming his true, *eternal self*.

Poetry is the *lord* of his *vineyard*, as art is the *lord* of Robert Bateman's *vineyard*, as music is the *lord* of Victor L. Wooten's *vineyard*; but Wooten was much more fortunate than many souls that are called to step into the *mesoteric* circle of life, because he had a personal mentor—a mysterious man called Michael.

Victor Wooten tells the story of how Michael came into his life, seemingly out of nowhere—which is how the omniscient guiding force of life works—to help Victor make the connection with the *Holy Flame of God*; and after much work in Michael's *vineyard* Victor makes the connection and is deemed worthy by Michael to pass his *holy flame* on to the world. This is how Victor describes the passing of the torch in his autobiographical novel *The Music Lesson, A Spiritual Search for Growth through Music:*

"Remember," Michael had said, "it is easy to learn to play your instrument, but playing it well is not enough. It is time for you to enter the world of a true musician. It is time for you to become an ally of Music and share her blessing. You are now a keeper of the flame. Please keep that flame alive, and do not, I say *do not* allow music to die."

When one is called by his *karmic destiny*, he has no choice but to share his *holy flame* with the world—whether one's *holy flame* is poetry like David Whyte, art like Robert Bateman, or music like Victor L. Wooten. One's *holy flame* is one's individual genius, the gift of his personal way that one receives as he lives his *karmic destiny*, and the more one shares his gift with the world, the more gifted he becomes. As Jesus said, **"For whosoever hath, to him shall be given, and he shall have more abundance; but whosoever hath not, from him shall be taken away even that he hath."** (Math. 13: 12)

I had broken the code of Christ's sayings, so I knew that he was making reference to the Spiritual Law of Attraction in that saying; that's why in my novel *Healing with Padre Pio* my alter ego Oriano said to Lorie, *"the more you give of yourself, the more of yourself you will have to give; and the less you give of yourself, the less of yourself you will have to give"*—which reflects the paradoxical reality of Christ's teaching of self-sacrifice.

That's why I made the virtue of giving central to my personal ethic, and why I *had* to write my novel *Keeper of the Flame;* because I, too, was called by my *karmic destiny*, and I really have no choice but to share my way with the world.

34. Letting Go and Letting God

"*All destiny leads down the same path—growth, love and service,*" said Elisabeth Kubler-Ross in her memoir *The Wheel of Life,* which speaks to the three stages of man's evolution through life: GROWTH in the *exoteric* first stage; LOVE in the *mesoteric* second stage, and SERVICE in the *esoteric* third stage.

The *exoteric* first stage of evolution is the selfish stage of evolution, because soul has to acquire self-identity to find its way back home to God—and find its way back to God it must, because like the acorn seed soul is teleologically driven to realize its divine nature. So in the first stage of evolution man's focus is on personal growth, and he will do everything he can to satisfy his insatiable primary need for self-identity.

The *exoteric* first stage of evolution belongs to the ego, the archetypal medium by which soul acquires self-identity; and the more *life force* (the I-consciousness of Soul) the ego gets from life the more energy soul will have to grow in self-identity.

Ego is the archetypal matrix of I-consciousness that soul projects upon the screen of life, and ego's primary function is to acquire the *life force*—which makes ego very selfish in its efforts to constellate the *life force* for soul's growth. It's all about "me" in the first stage of evolution, and not until one has grown enough to see that life can no longer satisfy his primary need for self–identity will he look for another way to nourish his soul—like the artist Jerry Wennstrom whose art no longer satisfied his spiritual hunger and he burned all his art and abandoned his life as he knew it and "let go and let God."

Jerry Wennstrom tells his incredible story in his book *The Inspired Heart, An Artist's Journey of Transformation*, which speaks to *soul's desperate cry for individuation* even more loudly than David Whyte's or Robert Bateman's, because Jerry had the courage to put his faith completely in God, and for fifteen years he lived on his faith alone totally dependent upon the Moment to provide for his existence.

As difficult as it was, Jerry Wennstrom found his way, and he had the courage to go out and live his *karmic destiny* just as David Whyte and Robert Bateman and all souls that are called to become *Keepers of the Flame*—because they had no choice.

"If you don't get it right in this life, you will just keep coming back until you do," said Paul Twitchell, author of *The Flute of God*; that's why I came back to live my same life over again—because I had missed a golden opportunity to get it right the first time, and I wasn't going to let it slip through my fingers this time; and I didn't.

This time around I found my path in Gurdjieff's teaching, which awakened me to the Word behind the words of Jesus, but despite the spiritual clarity of my spiritual path I still hit a brick wall and had to "let go and let God"—an unbelievable experience that has inspired my work-in-progress, an allegorical novel called *The Flip*.

Like Jerry Wennstrom, whose art had brought him as far as he could go on his path, my path had brought me as far as I could go, and like Jerry Wennstrom I was totally baffled as where to go next; so I, too, abandoned to God: I decided to let the flip of a coin make all of my big decisions for me—*heads I do, tails I don't!*

WHY BOTHER?

For six months I "let go and let God," which was the most courageous and foolhardy thing that I have ever done to find my true self; but the most peculiar thing happened near the end of those living-on-the edge months: I began to notice a strange pattern whenever I flipped my coin to let God decide what I should do. I began to notice that my coin always *coincided* with my gut feeling!

Whenever I felt in my gut that I should do something and flipped the coin to see what God had decided, the coin agreed with my gut feeling; and whenever I got the gut feeling that I shouldn't do something, the coin also agreed. Finally I said to myself, I don't need to "let go and let God" anymore; *I can make up my own mind!*

The flip was my *soul's cry for individuation*, and from the moment I stopped "letting go and letting God" the Way opened up to me as never before—because I had finally brought my *karmic destiny* into alignment with my *spiritual destiny!*

35. Growth, Love, and Service

In the Parable of the Good Samaritan the priest knew the Law of Moses—*Thou shalt love the Lord thy God with all thy heart, and with all thy soul, and with all thy strength, and with all thy mind; and thy neighbor as thyself*—and he was morally bound to stop and help the injured man by the side of the road; but he didn't.

The priest knew what the right thing to do was, but he didn't have the moral integrity to do it because he wasn't ready to step into the *mesoteric* circle of life and take evolution into his own hands; that's why he walked on by the injured man.

By not helping the injured man, the priest chose to remain in the *exoteric* circle of life where he would continue to grow through the natural process of karmic reconciliation; but had he chosen to help the injured man he would have aligned his *karmic destiny* with his *spiritual destiny* and taken evolution into his own hands by giving back to life.

In the *exoteric* circle of life, we take from life; that's what creates the karma that keeps us bound to the eternal cycle of life and death—because whatever we take from life we will one day have to pay back. And only when we start giving back to life can we break the cycle of life and death and realize our *spiritual destiny*.

The Levite was also a religious man, and though he may have known that it was only right to help the injured man, he didn't bother because he too wasn't ready to take evolution into his own hands. Like the priest, he was still a taker of life; and by his choice to not help the injured man he condemned himself to remain in the *exoteric* circle of life where he would be forced to grow through the natural law of karmic reconciliation.

The *exoteric* circle of life is the unconscious stage of evolution, because man does not know that he is subject to the Spiritual Laws of Karma and Reincarnation; and he will continue to grow in self-consciousness through the "hard knocks of life," as the expression goes, until he begins to see that he is the author of his own *karmic destiny*.

The Samaritan on the other hand was ready to take evolution into his own hands, because he had grown enough in self-consciousness to UNDERSTAND, as St. Padre Pio, would say, the moral imperative of helping his neighbor; and he nursed the injured man's wounds and took him to an inn and paid for his care.

By showing love for his fellow man, the Good Samaritan stepped into the *mesoteric* circle of conscious evolution, which Jesus called the *kingdom of heaven,* and he was on his way to realizing *eternal life*—because by giving love to the injured man he was paying life back for his own life that he owed to the natural process of karmic evolution.

As I said, I was born *mesoterically minded*, and I was ready to take evolution into my own hands; that's why I went on a quest for my true self. I found Gurdjieff, and with his teaching I began to transform the consciousness of my karmic shadow self until I had grown enough to see that I was the author of my own *karmic destiny*; that's when I started giving back to life, like offering the services of my trade to help restore St. Sylvester's Historic Mission Church on the Indian reserve in my hometown.

I volunteered six weeks of my precious summer work time painting the interior of the church, as well as supervising and helping on the exterior painting of the wooden siding; but all of my volunteerism bothered some people in my hometown.

When a woman from Nipigon learned that I was doing all of that work for nothing she said to me, "Are you crazy?"—because she did not UNDERSTAND that I was being paid in *virtue,* or what Jesus called "treasures in heaven."

"Lay not up for yourselves treasures upon earth, where moth and rust doth corrupt, and where thieves break through and steal. But lay up for yourselves treasures in heaven, where neither moth nor rust doth corrupt, and where thieves do not break through nor steal; for where your treasure is, there will your heart be also. The light of the body is the eye: if therefore thine eye be single, thy whole body shall be full of light. But if thine eye be evil, thy whole body shall be full of darkness. If therefore the light in thee be darkness, how great is that darkness! No man can serve two masters; for either he will hate the one, and love the other; or else he will hold the one, and despise the other. You cannot serve God and Mammon." (Math. 6: 19-24)

Jesus used the word "treasure" for *life force,* the precious I-consciousness of Soul that man needs to satisfy his spiritual hunger for total self-identity; and by two masters Jesus meant the lower and higher self. And when one stores one's "treasures upon earth," all Jesus meant was that one is nourishing his lower self with the *life force,* thereby incurring the wrath of karmic reconciliation—

WHY BOTHER?

"where moth and rust doth corrupt, and where thieves break through and steal" (all agents of the karmic process of reconciliation); and by storing one's "treasures in heaven," Jesus meant one nourishes one's higher self.

But it takes great wisdom to store one's "treasures in heaven," which I would never have realized had I not mastered Gurdjieff's technique of *non-identification*. This is the discipline of detaching oneself from the object of one's concern, whatever that concern may be (food, drink, sex, egoic need for attention, religious convictions, whatever); and the more one detaches oneself from the object of one's concern the more "treasures" he stores in "heaven" and individuates his two selves, and, in the words of Jesus ***"his whole body shall be full of light"***—meaning, spiritual consciousness.

And the more I grew in spiritual consciousness by mastering the art of giving (I loved picking blueberries for some of my elderly customers), the more conscious I became of my fellow man, and the more compassion I had; this is why every summer for seven years I volunteered my vocational skills of taping, painting, and texturing to Habitat for Humanity in Thunder Bay to help other volunteers build homes for needy people, which became the inspiration for my novel *On the Wings of Habitat, A Volunteer's Story*.

36. In Bad Faith

The most tragic person in the world is someone who lives their life with integrity but whose life is a lie, like the agnostic Christian. As I wrote in my novel *What Would I Say Today If I Were To Die Tomorrow?*—**"self-deception is our greatest threat to personal growth, happiness, and wholeness."** This was my dilemma, and I would never have found out that I was living my life in bad faith like the agnostic Christian had I not heard a voice in my mind ask me the question, *"Why do you lie?"*

This question pierced my soul and struck at the core of my *being* (and *non-being*) and I could not get it out of my mind, and thus began my quest for the answer to why I lied. But to answer this question I had to master another one of Gurdjieff's techniques—*self-remembering*. I had to discipline myself to remember myself in all circumstances, and the more I turned my attention inward, the more I hated what I saw!

Like writing poetry (I developed a "poetry muscle" by writing one poem a day for one hundred days, a creative discipline inspired by Robert Bly's book *Morning Poems*), I developed a "liar-detector muscle," and I began to catch myself in a lie more often than I ever imagined possible, which awakened me to another Gurdjieffian technique that I had to master (as far as it was possible to master), *non self-justification*—because more often than not whenever I caught myself lying I caught myself justifying my lie!

It just never occurred to me how often I lied, and how often people lie without realizing it. Gurdjieff said

WHY BOTHER?

something in Ouspensky's book *In Search of the Miraculous* that bothered me for years until I began to exercise my liar-detector muscle:

"To speak the truth is the most difficult thing in the world; and one must study a great deal and for a long time in order to be able to speak the truth. The wish alone is not enough. *To speak the truth one must know what the truth is and what a lie is, and first of all in oneself. And this nobody wants to know.*"

Thus began my obsessive compulsion to be truthful in thought, word, and deed; and the more truthful I became the more moral and ethical I had to be, and this awakened me to my false shadow self, and the false shadow selves of others—so much so that I even became acutely sensitive to the presence of the Father of Lies, the Archetypal Shadow—*which is why Jung said that it takes great moral integrity to see the shadow.*

That's how I was able to see the agnostic Christian's bad faith so quickly and why he never spoke to me again in the three years that he served as pastor for my hometown United Church. Aside from a polite hello, he avoided me like the plague.

37. A Voyage of Discovery

In one of my ten spiritual healing sessions that became the heart of my novel *Healing with Padre Pio*, St. Padre Pio told me that life was a voyage of discovery, which my relationship with him proved to be—because through him I discovered something about myself that would have taken years to discover on my own, if ever.

I went into my spiritual healing sessions with what the Canadian writer Robertson Davies called an "insolent assurance," an attitude born of my gnostic wisdom that I had painfully garnered living Gurdjieff's teaching of "work on oneself," my *Royal Dictum*, Christ's sayings, and a personal ethic distilled from my daily encounters with life (not to mention the blind spiritual conceit that I had assumed living "the most direct path to God"); but it didn't take long before I began to be humbled by the Ascended Spiritual Master who had suffered the pains of the crucifixion wounds of Jesus for fifty years.

In my second session I had the insolence to ask him a question in Italian, which took the spiritual sensitive who was channeling St. Padre Pio by surprise. I didn't translate for her what I was asking, because I was testing the whole process of channeling the Saint; but he took it all in stride. I wanted to know if he believed that Jesus had died on the cross for the sins of the world, because I believed that we are all responsible for our own karma; and this is what St. Padre Pio replied: *"I want him to know that what he is speaking of is trust. In order to leave all judgments behind, one must trust not only in oneself, but also in humanity, and in the*

WHY BOTHER?

greater good which is the good of all, and not just the self."

With this response began my humbling experience, and the more research I did on St. Padre Pio (aside from all the research that I did on the Internet, I read ten books on Padre Pio's life), the more humbled I was; and then it happened: while Penny and I were doing our daily spiritual contemplation in her office one evening I experienced the healing grace of St. Padre Pio's redemptive love which slew my vanity, and from that evening on I had a whole new relationship with the Ascended Master.

So devastating was the power of his healing grace that my vanity—which could withstand the most capricious winds of life—was ground to dust, and before my sessions were over I came to the astonishing realization that **our life is nothing more than a journey through vanity to humility**, and I asked him if he would work with me on another book because the Preacher's words—*"vanity of vanities, all is vanity"*—had opened up to me like the sayings of Jesus did when I broke the code of his secret teaching.

The theme of my sequel to *Healing with Padre Pio* was going to be about man's journey through vanity to humility, and he said he would. *"Our work is not done, my son,"* he replied; and I can't wait to begin my next voyage of discovery with the Ascended Spiritual Master who slew the insolent beast of my spiritual conceit!

38. The Great Slayer of the Real

I've been an initiate of my spiritual path for thirty-five years, ever since I dropped Gurdjieff's teaching; but it wasn't until I was humbled by St. Padre Pio's redemptive love that I saw through the spiritual conceit of "the most direct path to God."

"The mind is the vanity of all spiritual paths, without exception," I wrote in the last chapter of my novel *Healing with Padre Pio*, because regardless how pure the teachings, or how noble one's intentions, the mind has a way of always tripping us up.

"The Mind is the great Slayer of the real. Let the disciple slay the Slayer," said one of the sayings that I garnered in my quest for my true self—from *The Voice of the Silence*, by H. P. Blavastky; but one can spend his whole life trying to slay the Slayer and fail, because the Mind cannot be slain as long as we live in the physical world. The best that we can do is become masters of our own mind and not its servant.

When Penny and I moved to Georgian Bay and became members of our spiritual community in South Central Ontario I met a Higher Initiate from Southern Ontario who tried to put me in my place because I was only a Fourth Initiate and was speaking from the Mental Plane, as though what came from the Mental Plane was false knowledge. "Oh that's just mental knowledge," she said to me, with a dismissive wave of her hand when I supported my commentary with a quotation from one of my favorite writers.

WHY BOTHER?

In "the most direct path to God" a Higher Initiate is an initiate of the Fifth, or Soul Plane of Consciousness, which is the first of the Spiritual Worlds of God (there are many planes above this); all other initiations below the Fifth Plane take place in the material lower worlds—the Astral, Causal, and Mental Planes of Consciousness.

When we moved to Georgian Bay I was an initiate of the Mental Plane (I became a Higher Initiate two years later), but because I had already given birth to my spiritual self on the Soul Plane of Consciousness before I became a member of "the most direct path to God" I was open to the higher energies of Soul Consciousness to flow freely through me, as Jesus had promised with his teaching. This is how I wrote the first of my three "Soul talk" books, *The Way of Soul*, which pulled Carl Jung into my dreams.

"Spiritual wisdom is not predicated on one's level of initiation," I replied to this woman, who suffered OCD and had to wipe her chair and table top before sitting down in a coffee shop. *"One can be a First Initiate or a non-initiate for that matter and still be open to the Sound Current of God. Was Wordsworth a Higher Initiate? Was John Keats? Was Gandhi? Doesn't their wisdom count for anything? Surely you can't be that naive?"*

Jesus called the Sound Current the "water of everlasting life," which comes from God and flows through all of life and is open to everyone, not just initiates of "the most direct path to God," and I saw spiritual wisdom everywhere—especially in inspired works of literature; but that was the kind of vanity my spiritual path fostered with every initiation, and when one was blessed to become a Higher Initiate vanity had a way of making them feel superior to the rest of the community, and the world—not unlike the "Perfects" of the Cathars, a Gnostic Christian sect in Languedoc France in the 12th Century that was eventually wiped out by the Holy Roman Catholic Church.

When the Roman Emperor Constantine assembled all the bishops of the Christian churches to bring them all under one roof at the First Council of Nicaea in AD 325, the pure Gnostic teachings of Jesus Christ, which taught the principles of *eternal life* like the Parable of the Good Samaritan, were molded into the dogma that it has become today—which holds that our soul is created at the moment of human conception and that Jesus is the only begotten Son of God and only through Jesus Christ can we be saved.

That's the vanity that Christianity bred, which was the bane of my young life; so it doesn't matter which path we're on, the mind has a way of always tripping us up—even in the teaching of Buddhism whose primary function is to slay the great Slayer and in the process slays the spiritual self completely out of the Divine Plan of God!

But I was no less guilty of spiritual elitism than my fellow Higher Initiates; that's why I said to St. Padre Pio in my last session, "When I look back at my life before I began these spiritual healing sessions, I want to puke. *I want to just throw up!"*

I could almost hear him laughing, which he was according to the spiritual sensitive who was channeling him. "But you needed that to get here," he replied, once again giving me more food for thought…

39. The Selfish, Unselfish, and Selfless Self

The purpose of life is to create a new "I" of God. This is done through natural evolution. The new "I" of God is created through the natural process of karma and reincarnation. The atom of God, which comes from God for the specific purpose of growing and evolving into a God-realized Soul, has to go through three stages to complete its spiritual destiny. These stages are the selfish, unselfish, and selfless self.

The selfish self is realized in the *exoteric* circle of life, which is characterized by egoic growth, and it is all about taking from life; the unselfish self is realized in the *mesoteric* circle of life, which is characterized by integrating the inner and outer self, and it is all about giving back to life; and the selfless self is realized in the *esoteric* circle of life, which is characterized by service to life, and it's all about unconditional love.

Every soul has to go through the three stages of life. There are no exceptions. Once a soul has realized enough self-identity in the *exoteric* circle of life through the natural process of karmic reconciliation, it will gravitate to the *mesoteric* circle of life where it will take evolution into its own hands. Here the soul meets a teacher.

Taking evolution into our own hands means taking karmic responsibility for our life, which means living in harmony with the Spiritual Laws of life. This is the most demanding stage of soul's evolution, because it means transforming the consciousness of one's lower self. Here soul *"gathers and collects herself into herself,"* as Socrates expressed it in Plato's *Phaedo*; and soul redeems herself from her outer self.

Jesus called this stage the *kingdom of heaven*, and here one learns to "die" to his life to "save" his life, as Jesus expressed his *individuation process* of the two selves. It takes many lifetimes to enter the *kingdom of heaven* to "work" on oneself, but with each life that we "work" on ourselves we make it that much easier in our next life to become one whole self; so if we don't get it right in this life we will just keep coming back until we do. There is no fear of failure in the Divine Plan of God, and all ways are the right way for that soul. As St. Padre Pio said, "There is no one way."

When soul has individuated the two selves it will begin its life of service, and it will be born with a calling to serve God. This is the third and final stage of evolution where soul pays life back for its own life by serving God, and soul serves God by serving life with unconditional love, as Mother Teresa, Gandhi, Padre Pio and countless souls have done throughout history; and thus the Wheel of Life continues to spin in endless repetition as souls come into the world, grow, and return back home to God.

40. Why Bother?

Christ's teaching transcends time, which makes the Parable of the Good Samaritan a timeless teaching of *eternal life*. It does not matter if the priest and Levite were constrained by cultural and/or religious norms and could not stop to the help the injured man; Jesus was addressing soul's perennial need for *eternal life*.

Jesus did not judge the priest and Levite for not stopping to help the man who fell among thieves and was robbed and left half dead; he simply answered the cynical lawyer's question, "What shall I do to inherit eternal life?"

Jesus knew that not everyone that is called to the *kingdom of heaven* is ready to live the conscious spiritual life of the Way, but he gave his teaching to the world hoping that his spiritual seed would land on good soil:

"And he spake many things unto them in parables, saying, ***Behold, a sower went forth to sow. And when he sowed, some seeds fell by the way side, and the fowls came and devoured them up; some fell upon stony places, where they had not much earth: and forthwith they sprung up, because they had no deepness of earth: and when the sun was up they were scorched; and because they had no root, they withered away. And some fell among thorns; and the thorns sprung up, and choked them: But other fell into good ground, and brought forth fruit, some an hundredfold, some sixty-fold, and some thirty-fold. Who hath ears to hear, let him hear.***" (Math. 13: 3-9)

Christ's parables speak to one's level of consciousness. If one is *exoterically minded,* he will not hear the Word behind the words of Jesus, because his "soil" (consciousness) is not evolved enough to receive the "seed" (the Word); but if one is *mesoterically minded* he will hear the Word behind the words of Jesus, and his "soil" will be receptive to the "seed." This is what Jesus meant by those who had "ears to hear."

Many *exoterically minded* souls will receive the "seed" and try to make it grow, but the "seed" can only grow according to the conditions of the "soil." When I awakened to the Word within, I tried to sow the "seed," and it never failed to surprise me just how accurate Jesus was in his parable with respect to the conditions of one's "soil."

To receive the Word of God one has to be worthy of the *kingdom of heaven,* and one is worthy only when he comes to the realization that life can do no more to nourish his spiritual hunger for self-identity and his soul cries out for individuation.

By his own admission, Carl Jung wrote that by the age of forty he had "achieved honor, power, wealth, knowledge and every human happiness," yet he had lost his soul. *"My soul, my soul, where are you?"* Jung writes in his Black Book (leave it to Jung to make the classic *Jungian slip!*), and thus began Jung's historic "confrontation with the unconscious" and journey through the *mesoteric* stage of evolution.

The poet David Whyte was "rotting on the vine" of his professional life and his soul also cried out for individuation, *"Has anyone seen David?"* He heard the call and stepped into the *mesoteric* circle of life by taking up the life he was called to live, and his life began to flourish beyond his expectations. Robert Bateman heard the call when his soul asked, *"Is that it? Is that all there is to art?"* and his life flourished so far beyond his expectations that he became an active environmentalist and began giving back to life. And Jerry Wennstrom heard the call and out of desperation surrendered his life to God, living from day to day at the mercy of the Moment, and his life also flourished so far beyond his expectations that his art and life have become one today, and he too is giving back to life.

When a soul is called, it has no choice but to heed the call or it will suffer the agony of spiritual hunger; and not until one takes evolution into his own hands will he nourish his primary need for self-identity. So one can bother or not to stop and help the injured man by the side of the road; it's entirely up to him. If his need for spiritual growth is great enough, he will stop; and if not, he will pass on by.

There will always be an injured man by the side of the road, and there will always be travelers passing by; but only those travelers who are ready to enter into the *kingdom of heaven* will stop to help the injured man, because that's how life works. As St. Padre Pio likes to say, *"It is what it is."*

Plus an Interview With the Author and More

Insights

"To everything there is a season..."

Whenever I'm working on a new book the embryonic soul of my book pulls into itself all the material that it needs to grow and realize itself, and I've grown accustomed to all the coincidences that keep popping up whenever the soul of my new book is going through a growth spurt, which happened so often when I was writing *Healing with Padre Pio* (at least a dozen books were pulled into my creative field to expand my book's theme of my spiritual healing) that it was getting spooky; but I never expected that I would be told directly what book to read, which is precisely what St. Padre Pio did when he recommended that I read *Love Without End, Jesus Speaks*, by Glenda Green.

Jesus appeared to the artist Glenda Green so she could paint his portrait (which she did, titled *The Lamb and the Lion*), and out of Christ's many visitations with Glenda was born her book *Love Without End, Jesus Speaks*, which I read at St. Padre Pio's request; and, at the risk of taxing my reader's credulity even more than I already have with my relationship with the Ascended Master St. Padre Pio, I have no doubt that the spirit that appeared to Glenda Green in her studio was the real Jesus. It's immaterial to me whether anyone believes this or not; the point is that I believe it, and that's all that really matters—because, need I repeat myself; *life is an individual journey...*

WHY BOTHER?

In Chapter 13, "Pathways to Success", Jesus tells Glenda that we are here to further God's creation, ***"You were created in the likeness of God to extend the creative powers of our Father into all the dimensions in which you dwell, seek and create. Where you are is where your work unfolds. You are where you were meant to be,"*** and then he gives Glenda four principles that we need to succeed in our journey through life: (1), **Be the love that you are;** (2), **Do the right thing;** (3), **Follow life and the living;** and (4), **Forgiveness**.

As with all of Christ's sayings, these principles work in consort; so the more we live by one principle, the more we grow in the consciousness of the others. When Jesus tells us to be the love that we are, he is appealing to our higher nature; like the Good Samaritan who through his act of compassion for the injured man *did the right thing* and grew in the consciousness of his eternal life and the love that he was. The priest and the Levite chose not to help the injured man, thereby denying themselves the opportunity to grow in the spiritual consciousness of their eternal life and the love that they were.

I was fascinated by Glenda Green's book, because Jesus elucidated upon the secret teaching of eternal life that he couched in his sayings and parables to the point where he satisfied my need to know everything that I craved to know about his teaching, which brings me to the third principle that he gave Glenda: **Follow life and the living**.

Something about this principle intrigued me. Like most seekers, I sought my answers to life's questions in the ancient spiritual traditions of the world, little expecting to find my answers in the currents of daily life; and I did find my answers with the teaching that Gurdjieff had assembled from ancient sources, which he called the Work, the Fourth Way, the System, and "work on oneself". But I was one of the lucky seekers who broke the code of the secret teaching. Many seekers do not, and they are left with a sense of longing to know the meaning and purpose of life that can never be satisfied.

This is precisely why Gurdjieff said that there is only self-initiation into the mysteries of life—*because only by living the Way will the Way reveal itself to us!* And one does not have to go to the ancient spiritual traditions of the world to find the Way, because the Way is everywhere to be found—most especially in the creative currents of daily life as the poet David Whyte reveals with his book *Crossing the Unknown Sea, Work as a Pilgrimage of Identity,* and the artist Jerry Wennstrom with his book *The Inspired Heart,* and essentially all creative people who dare to heed the call to their *spiritual destiny* and true self!

"The third principle of success is so integral to life that most people overlook it as a basis of achievement and fulfillment: Simply follow life and the living!" said Jesus in Glenda Green's book *Love without End, Jesus Speaks.* **"The whole universe is built around a priority for life and the living. Therefore, you cannot afford to ignore this principle. Do not follow the dead and dying. By this I mean do not adapt to ways of life, structures, ideas, concepts, or businesses which are becoming ineffective and obsolete. Look for new alignments, opportunities, and understandings which refresh your life,"** added Jesus.

Glenda connected the dots and put the puzzle together: "As we follow life and the living, we move forward. Life is being created anew each day, and consciousness is expanding with every new burst of life.

WHY BOTHER?

This is not to say that our heritage should not be studied and honored. However, we cannot effectively navigate our lives through a rear-view mirror. We cultivate a true competency for living by adopting a forward approach to life while learning to value its potential for change and growth."

This is precisely what I did when I finally mustered my courage and learned how to use the Internet, which connected me with the currents of daily life, and I also learned how to self-publish my own e-books which is the coming wave; and this is precisely what I did when I went to an intuitive consultant for a spiritual healing. I listened to my inner voice and explored this whole concept of spiritual healing, and I was rewarded with an experience that changed the course of my life and brought my *karmic destiny* into much greater alignment with my *spiritual destiny* than I could ever have wished for!

And this is precisely what St. Padre Pio meant when he told me that the world needs to let go of the old and embrace the new (he was referring to the rigid dogma of religious thought, specifically the ancient tradition that he embraced when he was a humble Capuchin monk). As the Preacher, whose wisdom speaks for all ages, said: *"To everything there is a season, and a time to every purpose under the heaven"* (Eccl. 3: 1).

Preview of Coming Work

OLD WHORE LIFE

Exploring the Shadow Side of Karma

Spiritual Musings by Orest Stocco

Chapter 39

The Way of Soul In the Strange, Strange World of Dreams

A few months before the renowned psychoanalyst Carl Gustav Jung died, he wrote to an English correspondent: *"I have failed in my foremost task to open people's eyes to the fact that man has a soul, that there is a buried treasure in the field..."*

I met C.G. Jung in a dream one night. He came to me because he wanted to talk about my book *The Way of Soul*. This book wasn't published yet. It wasn't even transcribed. I had only begun transcribing the first chapter, but I got pulled into other projects and never completed the transcription of my remaining tapes, which would then have to be reworked and edited for publication; this is why I was so shocked when Jung held my book *The Way of Soul* in his hand and told me that he wanted to discuss it with me.

How I came to create *The Way of Soul* is a story in itself, which I have to relate to give context to my remarkable dream experience with Carl Jung. My spiritual musing today then is going to be on the way of Soul in the strange, strange world of dreams…

When I met Kevin Archer (the fictional name for the real life water color artist in my novel *The Waking Dream*) in the art gallery in Kildair (also a fictional name) in South Central Ontario, I was still processing all of the archetypal energy from the seven past-life regressions that I had just completed a month or so earlier.

In my fourth past-life regression I was brought back to the Great Ocean of Love and Mercy, which is the Body of God, where all atoms of God come from; and in the same regression I was brought back to my first primordial human life on earth when I experienced the birth of my reflective self-consciousness. I had such an explosion of consciousness because of my seven past-life regressions that I had to do something with all that archetypal energy, so I decided to do what I came to call a series of "Soul talk" books.

I decided to *let go and let Soul speak,* as it were (a technique somewhat akin to Jung's technique of *active imagination*), which became the inspiration for my three "Soul talk" books, starting with *The Way of Soul.* Every morning when I commuted to and from my work as a drywall taping and painting contractor I would talk into my mini recorder that I had hanging from my rear-view mirror, but I would not have done my three "Soul talk" books had I not met by pure "coincidence" Kevin Archer who had come to a depressing creative impasse in his art.

Providence brought us together. I need not expand upon this now because I have done so in *The Waking Dream* that was subsequently inspired by my three "Soul talk" books; suffice to say that Kevin was ready to meet his new teacher, true to the old saying that when the student is ready a teacher appears, and out of my mouth poured all the inspiration that he needed to break through his impasse and continue on his artist's way to wholeness.

I didn't know that I was the teacher he was providentially designed to meet, because I never saw myself as a teacher (my personal motto was: *let the world find its own way*); but I could not get over how quickly and easily it was for Soul to speak whenever I met him. It was like every time we met he had pressing questions that needed answers, and the answers just poured out of me like Christ's "water of everlasting life." *It was bizarre!*

I live by the principle that the more we give to life, the more we will get from life, which applies to everything that we do in life, and I shared with Kevin whatever wisdom I had garnered about the creative process from all my years of spiritual questing; and in some strange and mystical way we connected on a Soul level that opened the "tap" in me and there was no stopping the wisdom that flowed from my higher self, so Kevin got all the answers that he needed whenever *I let go and let Soul speak...*

Soul is the Consciousness of God, and as atoms of God our journey through life is to become aware of our divine nature; and the omniscient guiding force of life, which has been called Divine Spirit, the Way, the Word, Logos, Grace, Tao, Chi, Baraka, *élan vital* and many other names, is the Voice of God that guides us to our higher self by signs, symbols, coincidences, and whatever means necessary—like meeting someone who points us in the right direction just as Kevin Archer and I met in the new art gallery of Kildair!

WHY BOTHER?

Jesus called the Way the "water of everlasting life," which he said was in every person, and if we could tap into this "water of everlasting life" we would find our way and realize our divine nature. With Gurdjieff's remarkable teaching of "work on oneself," I learned how to tap into this spiritually quenching "water of everlasting life."

Actually, one cannot learn how to do this, as such; one can only realize it by *doing*, as Jesus said. *"Spirit cannot be taught, it must be caught,"* says the ancient saying. In other words, one has to *live* the Way for the way to reveal itself, and the more one *lives* the Way, the more the Way nourishes your spiritual self; and I *lived* Gurdjieff's teaching of "work on oneself; I *lived* Jesus Christ's sayings; I *lived* my *Royal Dictum* (my personal edict of self-denial); and I *lived* all of the wisdom sayings that I garnered from my daily life—which is how I could tap into the ineffable wisdom of Soul. (Incidentally, this is how I write all of my spiritual musings—*I just let go and let Soul speak!*)

In effect, it was my strange relationship with Kevin Archer that convinced me I had the gift of tapping into Soul consciousness; and so I decided to explore this gift and do a book by just *letting Soul speak.* This simply meant that I let go and let my higher self come through, which essentially is what all creative writers do when they write. That's how I created my book *The Way of Soul*, which Jung wanted to discuss with me in my dream.

My dream with Jung became central to my novel *The Waking Dream,* which was accepted by an American publisher but which I declined to proceed with because my editor and I did not have a meeting of minds; but all the same, my experience with C.G. Jung speaks to the way of Soul in the strange world of dreams—because Jung and I did talk about my book *The Way of Soul*, which was still a long way from being published yet!

So, what happened? Did I actually meet C.G. Jung in my dream? Or was he an archetypal manifestation of my own unconscious? That's the question that inspired today's spiritual musing—because I believe that both are true.

Carl Jung had a dream that puzzled him his whole life. He dreamt that he saw himself in a hillside chapel in a meditative posture dreaming his life as Carl Jung, and he *knew* that the man dreaming his life as Carl Jung was his real Self and that the psychiatrist called Carl Jung was his dream. In effect, *he knew that he was dreaming his own life!*

Jung's dream is reminiscent of the philosopher Chuang Tzu's famous dream: *"I dreamed I was a butterfly, flitting around in the sky; then I awoke. Now I wonder: Am I a man who dreamt of being a butterfly, or am I a butterfly dreaming that I am a man?"*

I had an experience that sheds light on both Jung's and Chuang Tzu's dream experiences. I woke up in my dream and became acutely aware of just how real everything was in my dream state. The reality of my dream state was a thousand times more real than my reality in my non-dream, physical state of consciousness; but I wanted to prove to myself which was the greater reality, so I woke up from my conscious dream experience to test my senses. I turned the light on in my bedroom and just sat on my bed and took in the reality of my physical state of consciousness, but it just didn't compare to the highly intensified reality of my dream state of consciousness; so I decided to go back to sleep and resume my dream state of consciousness, which I did. *I*

WHY BOTHER?

woke up again in my dream and concluded that my dream state of consciousness was more real than my physical state!

The secret knowledge of dreams teaches that dreams are a gateway to the Other Side; meaning, the parallel worlds of other dimensions. These parallel worlds are the other planes of consciousness known as the Astral, Causal, Mental, and Soul Planes.

This is what I believed, and why my understanding of dreams had a tendency to always want to usurp the Jungian interpretation of dreams—until I had a new awakening and realized that each interpretation was just another face of the same reality!

I did meet Carl Jung on the Other Side in my dream, and Carl Jung was also an archetypal manifestation of the collective unconscious; but how can this be?

Jung came very close to answering this question. He wrote "My life is a story of the self-realization of the unconscious." The unconscious for Jung was the unrealized Self, the central archetype of his psychology of individuation—what the whole evolutionary process of life was all about for him (and for me as well); that's why he came to me upon reading my book *The Way of Soul*, because he had a dying curiosity to know all about "the alpha and omega of the Self."

"What is the Self? Where does the Self come from? And where does the Self go?" he asked me in my dream, because he could not find a definite answer when he was alive; and we talked for hours. Maybe even longer than his legendary thirteen hour talk with Sigmund Freud upon first meeting face to face in Vienna (time on the Other Side is not relative to time on this side), and I woke up from my dream bursting with excitement because I was finally able to pay

Jung back for the spiritual solace of his wisdom—especially his remarkable insights into the psychological nature of evil, which he called the personal and collective shadow.

Carl Jung came into my life to help me resolve my problem with my shadow and the concept of evil that my Roman Catholic faith had saddled me with, and I came into his life to help him resolve his problem of the Self; and we talked about what I called "the Divine Plan of God" in my as-yet unpublished book *The Way of Soul*.

Since I've already explored this in *The Waking Dream,* I need not expound upon it in today's spiritual musing; suffice to say that what Jung called the collective unconscious, I understood to be the unconscious state of Soul. And as Jung saw the collective unconscious forever in the process of individuating the Self, I saw Soul forever in the process of individuating the consciousness of its divine nature; and both interpretations were merely different facets of the same reality that complimented each other.

Jung saw dreams from a psychological perspective, and I saw dreams from a spiritual perspective, but both spoke to the same reality of the Divine Plan of God; and this reality is the essential purpose of life—which is to expand the consciousness of God by giving birth to a new "I" of God (what Jung calls the Self) through the evolution of life.

To answer Jung's three questions then: What is the Self? Answer: Soul. Where does the Self come from? Answer: The Self is a Soul seed, which is an un-self-realized atom of God that comes into the world from the Body of God to realize its divine nature. Where does the Self go? Answer: back to God a fully-realized Soul Self.

WHY BOTHER?

And if I may pose one final question: Is life real or a dream? Answer: to quote my mentor Gurdjieff: *"There is only self-initiation into the mysteries of life!"*

The Making of a Novel

My novel *Healing with Padre Pio* came as a surprise, as have most novels that I have written. It's as though the novel chooses the writer, and if the writer is true to his Muse he will comply. How, then, did *Healing with Padre Pio* choose me?

Quite by "coincidence." I have put quotation marks around the word coincidence because I want to indicate that there is a hidden side to coincidence that we cannot see, but I have identified this hidden side, and I call it *the omniscient guiding force of life*.

In effect, the variables of my life converged when I met the intuitive consultant (she prefers to call herself an intuitive consultant instead of a psychic) who channeled the Ascended Spiritual Master St. Padre Pio for my ten spiritual healing sessions that became the core fact of my novel *Healing with Padre Pio*. The convergence of specific variables of my life *became* the coincidence that set free the idea for my novel, but it was entirely my choice to act upon this idea or not. This simply means that coincidences point to a certain direction, but it's always our choice whether we go in that direction or not.

I chose to act upon the idea for my new novel that was set free by the coincidence of meeting the intuitive consultant; so my ten spiritual healing sessions with her actually happened in the real world of space and time. She channeled St. Padre Pio, and the spiritual healing that my narrator Oriano Felicci experienced was real. It happened to me, Orest Stocco; but like the writer Francisco Goldman who wrote the novel *Say Her Name,* I also made up a story around the core fact of my spiritual healing novel.

WHY BOTHER?

The core fact of *Say Her Name* was the accidental drowning of Francisco Goldman's beautiful and talented wife Aura Estrada, and the core fact of *Healing with Padre Pio* was my ten spiritual healing sessions with St. Padre Pio. The rest is fictional narrative inspired by my life. But this begs the question; why not tell the story as memoir? Why couch the story in fiction? What is the advantage?

The Paris Review asked Goldman this very question: "You call this book a novel, but obviously many of the fundamental elements of the story are true. Could you talk a little about what you see as the relationship between fact and fiction in this book?" And the author replied: **"I made things up in order to be able to tell the truth."**

That sounds like a contradiction in terms. How can one tell the truth by making things up? That's not logical. Or is it simply another way of looking at the truth?

When Adrienne Rich was asked to define what poetry was, she replied: *"It is an act of the imagination that transforms reality into a deeper perception of what is."* That's what Goldman did: he transformed the reality of his relationship with Aura Estrada into a deeper perception of his reality with her; and this *deeper perception* gave us a better, more intimate understanding of his relationship with his beautiful young wife.

This is why I wrote my experience with St. Padre Pio as a novel and not a memoir—to get a *deeper perception* of my spiritual healing experience.

My intuitive consultant gave me a complimentary spiritual healing at her open house (by coincidence this was the day of my birth, making it a birthday gift whose benefit I could not have imagined!) which intrigued me enough to explore the whole concept of spiritual healing; that's what set free the idea for *Healing with Padre Pio*.

So the question my novel seeks to answer is this: **what is a spiritual healing?** And to answer it, I had to employ the creative power of my imagination to get a *deeper perception* of the concept of spiritual healing. This is my literary reason for writing a novel instead of a memoir. But I have to explain what I mean by this.

A novel is a thought process that creates its own reality. The writer feeds the story all the facts that he can assemble for his characters and story, and then he has to abandon to the thought process of writing—meaning, he lets the creative unconscious tell the story.

This is why writers are often surprised by their characters and where their story takes them. The story writes itself, as it were. As the Persian poet Omar Khayyam wrote, *"The moving finger writes, and having written moves on. Nor all the piety nor all the wit, can cancel half a line of it."* In effect, the writer has to trust the creative process.

Had I written a straight memoir of my spiritual healing experience, I would not have had the advantage of the creative unconscious to work out the answer to my question **what is a spiritual healing?** I would have had to puzzle the answer out myself. The creative unconscious is infinitely wiser than I am, so I abandoned to my Muse and let my story work out the answer for me, which it did. Once again, this act of creation is not unlike Jung's technique of *active imagination* which accesses the creative unconscious.

This is the magic of creative writing, and why writers get hooked on the process—because it gives us a *deeper perception* of what is!

WHY BOTHER?

Healing with Padre Pio was not an easy book to write. I had one session every month for ten months with my intuitive consultant, each lasting an hour and a half, and between sessions I read all the books that my sessions required me to read, and then I had to weave my fictional narrative in between and into the transcripts of my sessions; and transcribing the sessions was tedious work, not to mention editing them into reader friendly text.

The tricky part was weaving my fictional narrative into the text of my transcripts without violating the integrity of the experience; and the most difficult part of writing *Healing with Padre Pio* was making the whole story believable.

Only another writer will believe this, but writing what really happened was more difficult to make believable than what I made up! That's the irony of fiction. And I had to be very creative (and outrageously bold) to make my spiritual healing sessions with an Ascended Spiritual Master believable. This is how I went about it...

Padre Pio was a Capuchin monk living in San Giovanni Rotondo in Italy. He was the first Roman Catholic priest to suffer the holy wounds of Jesus, which are called the stigmata. He suffered the pain of the stigmata for fifty years.

Like Padre Pio, I was born Roman Catholic into a peasant family in southern Italy, and I also grew up with the desire of one day becoming a priest; but my faith began to waver, and finally I left the Church and became a seeker.

I found Gurdjieff's teaching, which transformed my life enough to open my windows of perception on the sayings of Jesus, and I developed a whole new relationship with Jesus Christ than the one I had as a Roman Catholic.

I believe in karma and reincarnation, so when I met St. Padre Pio who was being channeled by my intuitive consultant for my spiritual healing I took the opportunity to ask him all those questions that have haunted Roman Catholics for centuries; haunted most Christians, in fact. Questions like: does hell really exist? Can sins really be forgiven? Why does God allow so much suffering in the world? Do we only live one lifetime? Was Jesus the Son of God and sole savior of the world? Why did Jesus die on the cross? Did he really die on the cross? Because *The DaVinci Code* says otherwise. And so on.

The humble monk from San Giovanni Rotondo embraced his Roman Catholic faith with passion and implicitly believed the Roman Catholic doctrine; but Padre Pio was canonized shortly after his death. He was a Saint and Ascended Spiritual Master now. Was he as passionate about his Christian faith in heaven as he was on earth?

That's what I had to find out. And by asking him the tough questions I hoped to make my story as believable as I possibly could. I hope I succeeded, because all the questions that Oriano asks him were questions that tortured me growing up.

St. Padre Pio's answers surprised me!

An Interview with the Author

Conducted by Penny Lynn Cates

P: Why did you write *Why Bother? The Riddle of the Good Samaritan*?

O: It was unfinished business. I left the reader on the edge of a great mystery with my novel *Healing with Padre Pio* by ending my story with the question *Why Bother?* And it was only fitting that I address this; but in all honesty, I had no idea that it would turn out to be a book. This reminds me of Ernest Hemingway. He's quoted as saying that every one of his novels began as a short story that simply grew into a novel. I had planned to answer this question in a spiritual musing in the third volume of my Spiritual Musings series, but my Muse had other plans. Like Hemingway, I am also a servant of my Muse; and my musing just grew into a nice little book called *Why Bother?* There's another answer to your question. Like the Samaritan, you could say that I was also on my way to Jericho, and I saw a seeker stranded by the side of the road. He was dazed, confused, and disoriented; and I stopped to tend to him. Like so many birds in the Sufi allegory *The Conference of the Birds*, this seeker lost his way; and since I knew the way to Jericho I settled him down and assured him that I would help him find his way to Jericho; so in an allegorical sense, I'm just being a Good Samaritan to my fellow seekers by helping them find their way to Jericho.

P: What do you mean by Jericho?

O: That's a metaphor for the Way. Jesus called it the *kingdom of heaven*, which is not a place, as such; it's both a destination and one's path to one's true self. You could say that every soul is its own way to Jericho, but not every soul knows this; and all I've done with *Why Bother?* is inform my reader that to get to Jericho you have to connect with your inner self, which you can do by being true to your calling—whatever the calling may be. As I said in my book, David Whyte was called to poetry and he's on his way to Jericho. It's a tough road to Jericho, but the only way to get there is by having the courage to live your own life, like the artist Jerry Wennstrom who burned all his art and gave away his possessions and abandoned his life to the mercy of God. As you live your own life, you forge your own path; and one day you will see the lights of Jericho.

P: Will everybody find their way to Jericho?

O: Yes; because if we don't get it right in this life we will just keep coming back until we do. Like I said, there are no failures in the Divine Plan of God.

P: What did you hope to accomplish with this book? You told me on several occasions that you never know where your books are going to take you, but did you have a goal in mind when you wrote *Why Bother?*

O: I went into it hoping to answer the riddle of the Good Samaritan that I had posed in my novel *Healing with Padre Pio*, but it got a bit scary when I wrote the first chapter of *Why Bother?* because I honestly didn't know where my Muse was going to take me. After all, I got my answer to the riddle in the first chapter: *we have to have compassion for*

WHY BOTHER?

our fellow man to get to Jericho; but I had no idea that this was just an entry point into the mystery of Christ's teaching of eternal life, and I just went with it.

P: Now that you brought it up, what is Christ's teaching? I know I'm asking a lot, but for all those people out there like me who don't read the Bible, what do you think Jesus Christ's teaching is all about? Can you give us a Reader's Digest version?

O: That's exactly what I've done with *Why Bother?* It's a Reader's Digest version of Christ's secret teaching of salvation. The Parable of the Good Samaritan speaks directly to Christ's teaching of love, which is the central premise of his teaching. When all is said and done, unless we learn how to love our fellow man we will never get to Jericho.

P: Yes, I got that from your book; but it seems too simple.

O: I was watching a video on Carl Jung last night on the Internet. I'm doing research for my new book *The Summoning of Noman*, and Jung was talking about living the simple life in his lakeshore country home in Bollingen that he built with his own hands. He had no electricity or running water, and he had to cut his own firewood, pump his own water from the well, wash his own clothes by hand, and do his own cooking. He loved the simple life, but he said it was difficult to live the simple life. The same can be said about loving our fellow man. In principle it's very simple, but in practice it's the most difficult thing in the world to do; and the only way to find out why it's so difficult is to do it.

P: I think I know what you mean, but can you break it down for me please?

O: We're treading sacred ground here, but I'll try. Love is inherently self-transcending. When you give a person love you are giving them this precious energy that makes moral demands of them. They don't know moral demands are made of them, but they are affected by the inherently redemptive power of love, and this causes inner conflict. Love has the power to raise one's moral consciousness, and the more love you give to your fellow man the more you raise the moral consciousness of society, and society would prefer to stay where it is—firmly ensconced in the complacent status quo. Too much love can be dangerous. Look at what happened to Jesus. Just read the biographies of some of the world's great souls, starting with the "gadfly" Socrates who was condemned for corrupting the youth of Athens with his "seditious" philosophy, and President Lincoln who freed the slaves and was assassinated, and Mahatma Gandhi who liberated India from the yoke of Britain; he was also assassinated. The world is full of great souls who suffered for their love of man. Love can be dangerous because it's spiritually liberating. That's why Oriano tells Lorie in *Healing with Padre Pio* that one has to be wise as a serpent and gentle as a dove when giving love. Incidentally, this is why people say that love can turn on you. It's not love that turns on you, as such; it's the shadow that turns on you, because the shadow does not want to see its moral deficiencies in the mirror that you hold up to it with your love. That's why the Parable of the Good Samaritan pricks our conscience. Look at how the people of our hometown up north turned on us when my book *What Would I Say Today If I Were To Die Tomorrow?* came out.

WHY BOTHER?

As you know only too well, it was no picnic for us when I held the mirror for our town to see its own shadow. Like Padre Pio said, I chafe people with my honesty. Even members of our own spiritual community down here spitefully turned on me because they didn't like what they saw in the mirror that I held up for them with my uncensored candor, especially some Higher Initiates. Some members have a hate on for me that makes one wonder how they could be on this path of love. It gives one pause. But that's life, and I understand; so I have no rancor.

P: I wondered how you felt about that. Can you elaborate?

O: Should I?

P: Maybe you shouldn't, but you're also a Higher Initiate and I'm curious to hear what you have to say about this spiritual path. You say in your book that it's called the most direct path to God. Do you think it's the most direct path to God?

O: I've given this a lot of thought and I'm not so sure now. I used to be sure before I wrote *Healing with Padre Pio,* but I have mixed feelings now. Direct or indirect, what difference does it make when Soul has forever to find its way to Jericho? The point is that Soul is trapped in the cycle of karma and reincarnation, but it makes no difference when Soul finds its way out because Soul exists in the Eternal Present, or what Jesus calls the Holy Now in Glenda Green's book *Love without End, Jesus Speaks.* Time is moot from this perspective. If you want to know what I really think of this spiritual path, I would have to say that it has erected an invisible fence for its members; and by invisible fence I mean that they are fenced in by the spiritual conceit of this boast that it is the most direct path to God. It's like saying, there are many paths to Jericho but our path will get you there the quickest because we have the Inner Master who connects us with the Holy Current of God; but given that the only way to Jericho is through the path of your own individuation process, this could very well be an empty boast if one does not realize that it is an individual path and the Inner Master your higher self. This path may well speed up the individuation process, but one can speed up the individuation process with any path. Look at Padre Pio. He sped up his individuation process by embracing Christ's suffering the way he did. I also sped up my individuation process with Gurdjieff's teaching of "work on oneself" and my *Royal Dictum,* which I vowed to keep for the rest of my life. I didn't have to because it served its purpose much sooner than I expected, but the point I'm making is precisely what St. Padre Pio said, that life is a journey of the self; and direct or indirect, we will all find our way to Jericho some day because all paths lead back home to God. And if this tears down the invisible fence of that specious boast, maybe that's a good thing. Personally, I like this path for its comprehensive understanding of the Way; but I had a dream several weeks ago that may well be telling me it's time to move on.

P: Move on? Where to?

O: "The journey home to God is a flight of the alone to the Alone," said Plotinus.

P: So you're not fenced in, then?

WHY BOTHER?

O: Not any more. We all make our own fences. That's what *Healing with Padre Pio* is all about. I had no idea that I had erected such a fence around myself, but I did; and had I not had the good fortune to work with St. Padre Pio to heal my wounded Christian soul, I don't know how long I would've stayed caged in by the invisible fence of my own vanity. Maybe that's why I was compelled to write *Why Bother?* It brings some clarity to this issue of the invisible fences of vanity that our mind has a tendency to erect around us.

P: Can you tell me about your dream?

O: I was on a train that had just pulled out of the station platform of what I knew to be our spiritual community. I had just gotten on the train and was staring out the window. The grounds of our community were impeccably kept, beautiful lush green lawns, flowers, trees, shrubbery, and a beautiful small lake with benches here and there; and the building was made of stone with beautiful arched windows and doors, and it covered one third of the community grounds; but as the train pulled away from the community I got the strangest feeling from some of the members watching the train go by that they couldn't understand why I was leaving. But as beautiful and safe and secure as our spiritual community was, I couldn't help but feel that we were all prisoners of our own vanity, and it was time for me to move on. I felt sad for leaving, but I was also relieved that I had finally made the decision to leave our community prison of spiritual freedom. *"Parting is such sweet sorrow,"* said Shakespeare; that's how I felt as my train pulled away from our spiritual community.

P: This comes as a surprise.   Are you going to move on?

O: Probably, but not until the current spiritual leader passes on the mantle. When he does, if I'm around to see it, there's going to be a radical shift in the spiritual focus of this teaching; and that's going to be traumatizing. But that's not up for discussion.

P: Are you working on anything now?

O: Yes, my new book *The Summoning of Noman*. Something St. Padre Pio told me in one of my spiritual healing sessions really piqued my curiosity. He told me that I have relived my same life over again three times, and this is one of those times. The first time I lived my life as Orest Stocco I wasn't happy with the outcome, so I returned to relive my same life again for a different outcome, and I'm writing a book to explore my parallel life. This is radically new information about reincarnation. I've never heard of this before, reliving one's life over again to achieve a different outcome; but the more I explore this concept of parallel worlds, the more I believe that I was reborn into my same life to achieve a different outcome.

P: What outcome would that be?

O: To break the cycle of karma and reincarnation. I should have, but I didn't do it the first time around. This time I found the Way; and that, as Robert Frost said in his poem *The Road not Taken,* has made all the difference:

> "Two roads diverged in a wood, and I—
> I took the one less travelled by,
> And that has made all the difference."

Other Books by Orest Stocco

Healing with Padre Pio
Just Going With the Flow,
   And Other Spiritual Musings
Keeper of the Flame
My Unborn Child
What Would I Say Today
   If I Were To Die Tomorrow?
On the Wings of Habitat, A Volunteer's Story

Coming Works

Old Whore Life: Exploring the Shadow Side of Karma
Jesus Wears Dockers: The Messiah Secret Revealed
The Seeker: Quest for the Lost Soul of God

About the Author

Orest Stocco was born in Panettieri, Calabria, Italy. He emigrated to Canada and studied philosophy at university. A student of Gurdjieff's teaching for many years which opened him up to the Way, his passion for writing inspired such innovative works as *What Would I Say Today If I Were To Die Tomorrow?, Keeper of the Flame,* and *Healing with Padre Pio.* He lives in Georgian Bay, Ontario with his life mate Penny Lynn Cates. His personal dictum is: *life is an individual journey.* Visit him at: http://www.oreststocco.com

Spiritual Musings Blogs:
http://www.spiritualmusingsbyoreststocco.blogspot.com
http://www.letterstoascendedmasterstpadrepio.blogspot.com

ME AND MY SISYPHEAN ROCK

www.ingramcontent.com/pod-product-compliance
Lightning Source LLC
Chambersburg PA
CBHW051802040426
42446CB00007B/471